Khot-La-Cha

Khot-La-Cha

THE AUTOBIOGRAPHY OF

CHIEF SIMON BAKER

Chief Khot. la-cha;
Kind ♡ Heart

COMPILED AND EDITED BY

VERNA J. KIRKNESS

Douglas & McIntyre
Vancouver / Toronto

94 95 96 97 98 5 4 3 2 1

Douglas & McIntyre
1615 Venables Street
Vancouver, British Columbia V5L 2H1

Canadian Cataloguing in Publication Data

Baker, Simon, 1911-
Khot-La-Cha

ISBN 1-55054-157-9

1. Baker, Simon, 1911- 2. Indians of North America—British Columbia—Biography. 3. Squawmish Indians—Biography.
I. Kirkness, Verna J., 1935- II. Title.
E78.B9B34 1994 971.1'004979 C94-910582-1

Editing by Barbara Pulling
Cover design by Jim Skipp
Cover photograph by Gary Fiegehen
Text design by Arifin A. Graham, Alaris Design
Typeset by Brenda and Neil West, BN Typographics West
Printed and bound in Canada by D. W. Friesen & Sons Ltd.
Printed on acid-free paper ∞

The publisher gratefully acknowledges the assistance of the Canada Council and of the British Columbia Ministry of Tourism, Small Business and Culture for its publishing programs.

Proceeds from the sales of this book will be used to set up the Khot-La-Cha Scholarship Fund for First Nations students at the University of British Columbia.

I pray and give my thoughts to all of my people,
young and old

CHIEF SIMON BAKER

Contents

Acknowledgements

Simon and I are indebted to Simon's family for their interest and support during the writing of this book. In particular, we thank Emily, Simon's wife, for helping him to recall certain details of his life, for listening critically and patiently to draft after draft of the manuscript, and for the tea breaks she provided during our many taping sessions. We are grateful to Faye Halls and Nancy Nightingale, two of Simon's daughters, who assisted us by reading various drafts and contributing invaluable information.

We thank my colleagues Sheena Selkirk Bowman, Marcy Jackson, Wendy Wickwire and Kathy Morven, who came to my rescue in the fall of 1992 to help me continue with the book. At various stages throughout my work on this project, which began in 1986, I felt frustrated because the demands of my job left me little time to devote to the book. It meant a lot to me to have the willing help and support of colleagues. Sheena's assistance included getting the book proposal together. Marcy interviewed Simon about some aspects of his life, particularly those to do with playing lacrosse and being an elder. Wendy read drafts of the manuscript from early on and provided me with sound advice and encouragement. Kathy painstakingly and efficiently typed the manuscript. Their contributions were due to the high regard in which they hold Chief Simon Baker.

We acknowledge with thanks Lawrence Baker and Vanessa Campbell for the Squamish text they provided; Glen Newman of the Squamish Nation for the respect and consideration he has shown Simon over the years; and the Squamish Band for providing us with some audiotapes.

We are indebted to any and all of you who spurred us on by asking, "Well, how is the book coming?"

Finally, we thank the Creator for giving us the health and strength to complete this part of our journey.

Verna J. Kirkness

Introduction

Simon Baker is an ambassador of his own culture and of the human spirit." I don't think there could be a more fitting description of Chief Simon Baker, and I am indebted to the Sechelt Nation for this accolade, which they bestowed on Simon when they made him an honorary chief in 1985. It became, in my mind, the theme for his autobiography.

I believe it was in 1985 that Simon first broached the subject of having the story of his life written. He said to me, "I would like to tell about my life, what I've seen, what I've done, so my grandchildren and their children will learn of things that happened in this last hundred years. I believe that my story will be interesting for schools. I know when I go to schools today, kindergartens or even high school, the children like to hear about my life. They enjoy my songs that my elders taught me many years ago. I sing to them in my language and often I tell them the story of my people, using my talking stick."

I had known Simon long enough to know that he had a lot to share, and preserving his story in a book appealed to me. In 1986, we got down to work. Simon had broken his ankle while getting out of his hot tub, and his recovery kept him at home unable to do much but read. I suggested that he begin taping the events, experiences and memories he wanted in his autobiography.

He set up his tape recorder in his den and began to reminisce. He was very diligent about it. His story covered many highlights, but he always returned to memories about his grandmother, Mary Capilano; his time at boarding school; lacrosse; the powwows he had put on; and his trips abroad, especially to Germany. Sometimes we would hold taping sessions where I would interview Simon about particular aspects of his life. Simon is a master storyteller who loves to recount his experiences and to state his beliefs firmly in his own words.

Over the years Simon had kept a giant scrapbook, a three-foot by three-foot wallpaper advertising portfolio with a handle. In it were news clippings and photos, some dating back to the 1930s. The scrapbook provided me with a good clue as to what Simon prized most in his life. There were pictures of his grandmother, plenty of lacrosse photos, pictures of Simon in different countries. The scrapbook also included a number of photographs of Simon in full prairie headdress. He enjoys wearing the distinctive prairie headdress he was given when he was made an honorary chief of the Blood Indians of Alberta. By wearing the headdress, he feels he is honouring his prairie brothers.

I first met Simon at the National Indian Cultural Conference in Ottawa in 1970. I felt very honoured to be one of the twenty-five Indian delegates invited to attend this gathering. At the time, I was a curriculum consultant in Indian education for the Manitoba Department of Education. We were just launching a pilot project in Cree language immersion in a number of schools. I remember sharing with the group at the conference the importance of recognizing our Native languages in schools and facilitating our children's learning by using their first language as the medium of instruction. In those days, many children, particularly in the North, were fluent in their Native languages.

This national conference was a sign of changing times for our people. The year before, Prime Minister Pierre Elliott Trudeau had proposed a new Indian policy designed to abolish the special status of Indians. The government's White Paper evoked much reaction from Indians all over the country. While

Trudeau spoke of the policy as a move towards "a just society," it was interpreted by our leaders as a move towards "a society just for white people." There was definite disagreement with the government's direction and our people were speaking out about it. Ironically, Jean Chrétien was the Minister of Indian Affairs and Northern Development at the time. Chrétien had to learn some quick lessons about Indian history and culture while under attack for his government's proposed policy. It was then that he met such leaders as Simon Baker. To this day, he is known to Simon personally as a long-time associate.

The changing times of the late sixties had seen the appointment of Dr. Ahab Spence, a Cree originally from Manitoba, as head of the Cultural Development Section of the Department of Indian Affairs and Northern Development. Dr. Spence, Jean Goodwill, who was employed by the same department, and Ken Goodwill, of the Citizenship Branch of the Department of the Secretary of State — all Indians — were instrumental in organizing this first national conference on culture. Finally our voices were being heard in Ottawa.

The three-day conference allowed us to share our knowledge and to consider how we could revive, promote and preserve our cultures. Simon, I recall, played a prominent role. He chaired part of the conference and was helpful to all of us as he encouraged us to do whatever we could to deal with the loss of our languages, our customs and our peoples' traditional ways of making a living. He urged us to talk to our elders, to learn our ways and to pass on these teachings to the younger generation.

Simon told the delegates that his Squamish name is Khot-La-Cha, which means "Man with a Kind Heart." The name, given to him by his paternal grandmother, Mary Jacob, goes back three generations. Anyone who knows Simon will agree that he indeed has a kind heart. At the conference he instructed us on how to say his name properly. "Imagine that you have swallowed a fish bone and that it is lodged in your throat," he said. "The sound you make to dislodge it would help you to say 'Khot,' as in Khot-La-Cha." He also explained that the word "Squamish" means "the winds forever blowing," which I later learned to be very much the case on the West Coast.

In the conference report I prepared for the Curriculum Branch, I said it was apparent that the participants shared a national cultural bond, a bond linked to our basic values and our respective philosophies regarding the progress of our people in the general society. Today, Simon remembers that conference as a breakthrough in recognizing Indian culture.

It would be eleven years before I would meet Simon again. In 1981, I moved to Vancouver to work at the University of British Columbia as the Supervisor of the Native Indian Teacher Education Program (NITEP). The program had started in 1974, as had many other Indian teacher education programs in Canada. I had been involved in the creation of such programs in Manitoba, and have always been a strong advocate for Native teachers. Back in 1954, when I began teaching, there were probably fewer than fifty Native teachers in all of Canada. I believe that Native teachers are critical to the realization of quality education for our people. Not only are we role models, but because of birthright and experience we are able to relate to identity, culture and the traditions that must form the basis of our peoples' education.

The North Vancouver NITEP Centre was hosting the orientation program for NITEP students that year. Faye Halls, Simon's daughter, was the secretary for the program. Simon lived just a few blocks away, and he became a frequent visitor to the centre. It was there I had the great pleasure of meeting him again. He was very happy that I had come to Vancouver to work.

I began to invite Simon to various functions at the university. The students enjoyed his presence because he is such a jovial person. He loves to joke around, tell stories, sing with his drum and dance. Almost every gathering he leads ends with the deer dance, which leaves everyone laughing. He was soon acknowledged as a NITEP elder.

In 1984, Simon was made an honorary NITEP graduate in recognition of his outstanding service and dedication to the program. He was very proud of this honour, which was given in the year that his own granddaughter, Angela McDonald, received her Bachelor of Education degree through NITEP.

Simon took a keen interest in Angela's training and provided her with any artifacts, crafts or books she might need to help children better understand Native people and their culture.

It was appropriate that Simon should become an honorary teacher graduate. His commitment to the teachings of his grandmother, his grandfather, his parents, his uncle Chief Mathias Joe, elder Dominic Charlie and many others has made him a teacher in his own right. For him, it is part of his daily life to teach. He is no stranger to classrooms, either. He has visited schools all over the world for many years demonstrating his culture to the students and trying to instill in them a respect for one another. Angela has been teaching in Surrey since her graduation, and Simon still visits her school on occasion.

It is difficult to imagine what my life in Vancouver would have been like without the friendship of Simon and Emily and their family. The first thing a frequent visitor to their home notices is the closeness of the family. Simon and Emily have nine children, thirty-four grandchildren and twenty-four great-grandchildren. Their family is growing all the time. It is an advantage that most of their children, grandchildren and great-grandchildren live in the Vancouver area. So they enjoy many family celebrations together — birthdays, anniversaries, weddings, Mother's Day, Father's Day, Christmas and Easter. They are a very close-knit family.

At a gathering in 1993 where Simon was honoured as the recipient of the Brock House Society Senior Award, his daughter Faye used the analogy of a giant oak tree to describe her father. She said,

> I look at my father's life like a giant oak tree. He is the trunk, growing stronger and adding another layer of wisdom as every year goes by. As the tree grows and the branches spread out, he starts to touch other peoples' lives with his accomplishments. The trunk is now solid and full of strength and its branches are growing and reaching out to people, spreading his great wisdom and goodwill. At the base of this great tree are the roots, my mother, holding the tree and its branches together.
>
> Over all these years of achievements and accomplishments he has not forgotten the most important thing of all, those nine

main branches, his children. He has continued to nourish those nine branches with love, wisdom, strength, humour and, most of all, courage.

So now we have this great eighty-two-year-old tree. It towers over all the others and everyone looks up to it with admiration and awe. Its trunk is a tower of strength and its leaves are flying everywhere, reaching out and enriching so many lives. This tree has grown to have nine strong branches, thirty-two branches off those, and another twenty-two twigs off those smaller branches. Every one of those branches, down to the smallest twig, has been constantly nourished over the years by this great trunk and its roots. Now they are all full of love, strength, tradition, wisdom and, most of all, pride.

I have great admiration for Khot-La-Cha, this man with whom I have been closely associated over the past thirteen years. As well as being a friend, he has been my mentor. As a Cree from Manitoba, it has been important for me in my own work in Vancouver to have the wise counsel and support of respected elders in the area. Simon, Minnie Croft, originally from Haida Gwaii, and Vince Stogan from Musqueam played a major role in the progress we were able to make to expand the opportunities for our people at the University of British Columbia. These three elders share the distinction of being honorary NITEP graduates. They saw us through the challenges of establishing and implementing the Ts"kel Graduate Program and the First Nations House of Learning, and of building a Longhouse on campus, as well as participating with us in our day-to-day activities. Their presence gave us the confidence to forge ahead.

I loved the opportunity to be with these three elders, because they are so much fun. There were many occasions when I'd make my swing around to pick them up for a meeting. Usually I went for Simon first, then I'd pick up Minnie and go on to Musqueam for Vince. During the ride, I'd hear about their latest activities and all the other things they were involved in. Once we arrived, our meetings began with a prayer, then we'd have coffee with cookies or doughnuts. Simon always said he wouldn't work unless he was fed first. If it was a morning meeting, we'd often go to the Faculty Club for lunch afterwards. The jokes and stories continued, and we'd have a lot of laughs.

I have learned something about lacrosse in these past few years by attending a few of the North Shore Indians' Senior B lacrosse games with Simon. You can see that the young players are glad to have him there. This year, the team won the coveted President's Cup, and now they have joined the Senior A lacrosse league once again. In the May 11, 1994, issue of the *North Shore News*, sportswriter Jim Kearney published an article about "the reincarnated North Shore Indians lacrosse team." According to Kearney, "Those original Indians were Vancouver's most popular team — of any sport — in the Dirty '30s, when mass unemployment stalked the land and a mere 25¢ would get you a seat to see them play at the now long-gone Denman Street Arena. It burned to the ground late in the summer of 1936, but before it did the guys from the North Shore — half of whom, it seemed, carried the name Baker — regularly filled its 10,000 seats. At 83 and still a lively, crackling personality, Simon Baker remains the only living member of those long-ago teams."

I also got to visit the B.C. Lacrosse Hall of Fame in New Westminster. It continues to irritate Simon that Andy Paull, a player, manager and coach of the North Shore Indians during their heyday, didn't make the Hall of Fame.

I've enjoyed going to the racetrack with Simon and Emily as well. There is a ritual to these occasions. We arrive at the track around 5:30 P.M. and have dinner in the cafeteria while studying our racing forms. At 6:30, it is post time. Taking into account what the racing forms say about the horses and the jockeys, and how the horses look as they are ridden past us before the race, we place our bets. We don't tell each other which horses we are betting on. We usually favour those that have names like Fire the Council, Count the Indians and Captain Apache. Simon is inclined to pick horses like Promise Me Honey. We are still waiting for the owner of Khot-La-Cha, a young horse that Simon named, to run. Simon told me, "Last I heard, the horse named Khot-La-Cha finally got broken. It was hard because he was either too wild to saddle up or he'd just decide to lie down. I believe his name suits him."

Since meeting Simon again, I have been to totem-pole raisings where he dedicates the poles, to conferences and meetings where he makes presentations, to dinners in his honour, and to Simon and Emily's fiftieth wedding anniversary celebration, where he attempted to redeem himself by buying Emily a beautifully carved gold bracelet. (As you will read in this book, Emily had to buy her own wedding ring back in 1934.) In June of 1994, the Squamish Nation held a traditional Coast Salish ceremony to mark Simon and Emily's sixtieth anniversary.

Simon has often said, "I love to go out; I love to meet people. It is good medicine for me." This is obvious as we witness his determination to keep going even though he is now eighty-three years old.

Last year Simon told me he had been to visit his doctor. "The doctor told me I better slow down, that I'm an old man now," he said. "I couldn't believe it. I knew I was getting old, but I never thought of myself as an old man."

That is probably the secret to his long life.

While this book is about Simon, it is also very much about his wonderful wife of sixty years. Emily, like Simon, has tremendous energy. Though their interests differ somewhat, they have both contributed much to their people and to the well-being of society in general. Emily appears shy and quiet to the unsuspecting observer, but she wields a lot of influence over this six-foot, very outgoing man. The saying "Behind every good man is a good woman" certainly holds true for this couple.

Emily is such a gracious woman, and she keeps very busy. At seventy-nine, she still sews constantly. There is always a birthday coming up — sixty-five a year for the children, grandchildren and great-grandchildren alone. Recently Emily sewed three bridesmaid dresses and made her own outfit, complete with hat, for one of her granddaughter's weddings. Emily has a raspberry patch and apple trees in her back yard. She freezes and cans the fruit from these, along with plenty of salmon. She attends to her many flowers in the yard. And although she has now sold her store, Khot-La-Cha Arts and Crafts, to her daughter Nancy, she still works there on a part-time basis. She is truly amazing.

A couple of years ago Emily and Irene, Simon's sister, went to visit a palm reader. They came home all excited about how good the psychic was, how she had told them of things that really had happened in their lives and given them a glimpse of the future. They encouraged Simon to go and see her. At first, he said he had no intention of going, but later he decided it would do no harm, especially if no one knew about it. So he went on his own. The psychic told him, "You're dealing with the area of status most in your life, not just status for yourself but for your whole group. The people around you are as important, more important, in fact, than yourself; so this is a group status. You are concerned with family and larger groups at the moment. Environment — you wish you could go out and do more. You are quite limited in what you can do now compared to what you could. Whatever has happened to you in your life, you've kept a very realistic perception of the world. You're a strong leader. Pride of self is very high; you don't let yourself down.

"You're very blunt. This is a Sherman-tank thumb. You tell people exactly what you feel; you're straightforward and you've had lots of energy. I see this hand do a lot of things like go logging and fishing. You've got an unusual mind-line here with a cross on it. That's called a mystic cross. It's a psychic mark. When a person gets a cross in the middle of the hand, they have to help people. They don't just do it — they have to. That's a sign of a person who helps. This is what you're supposed to do all your life. Courage is in here, coming from your family. In your genetics there were people that had the courage to do what they had to do and you are like them. There is a grandmother here who influenced you a lot, on your mother's side of the family. You're a person not afraid to speak out, put forward ideas, be aggressive, tell the truth about matters. That's very strong in you and you're very analytical. Common-sense business you do well at. You have a sense of duty towards the aging here in the community. Looking after older people is within your hand, caring for people both in wisdom in the common every-day business sense and in the spiritual sense. It shows you have an understanding of the psychology of the human being. Your energy level is very strong all your life."

I feel she summed up Simon very well.

As Simon and I worked through his life experiences, I could see the influence of his grandmother, Mary Capilano, from whom he learned what it means to be Squamish. He learned the values he must uphold and the responsibility he must maintain as the father of the Capilano family. I see in him something too of his uncle Mathias Joe, who loved to perform the Squamish songs and dances, and who spoke with much humour. As well, I see in Simon the qualities of the great Andy Paull, as Simon often refers to him. From Andy Paull, he gained a love for sports and an understanding of politics.

Friends, readers, we give you in this book the story of Simon Baker, the husband, the father, the grandfather, the great-grandfather. We give you a leader, a spokesman, a diplomat and an elder. We give you an advisor, a teacher, a counsellor, a friend. We give you a lacrosse player, a smooth waltzer, a longshoreman, a carver and, now, a storyteller. Enjoy his story, for he is truly an ambassador of his own culture and of the human spirit.

Verna J. Kirkness

1

THE EARLY DAYS

The Princess of Peace

I am the grandson of Chief Joe Capilano and Mary Agnes Capilano. They were my mother's parents. There is a great story behind each of my grandparents. My grandmother, Mary Capilano, held the title of the Princess of Peace.

I was told by her that for many years the Squamish and the Yaculta Indians, two very powerful southern B.C. coastal tribes, were fighting each other. They used spears and muskets to try to kill each other. They were fighting for rank, honour and respect for their tribe.

She said her grandfather, Chief Payt-sa-mahk, and his brother George Capilano wanted to make peace with the Yacultas to make their territory safe for their people. Her grandfather took one hundred war canoes, each with twenty men, to where the Yacultas lived to ask for peace to stop the many years of fighting. They spent two days trying to get the Yacultas to believe that they really wanted peace. Finally, her grandfather ordered all the men to throw their spears into the water and to empty their muskets by firing them into the water. That's when the Yacultas believed that the Squamish were there in peace, so they got rid of their weapons, too.

My grandmother's grandfather, Payt-sa-mahk, had several wives. One of his wives was an Indian princess of the Nicomen Indians of the Lower Fraser. They had a son, Skauk-kal-ton.

The Yaculta chief had a daughter, Say-pul-kath. Skauk-kal-ton and Say-pul-kath were married. Now there were blood ties to keep the peace between the two tribes at last. The first child of Skauk-kal-ton and Say-pul-kath was Líxwlut (Mary Agnes), known as the Princess of Peace. I believe her name means great lady, leader.

I spent a lot of time with my grandmother, Mary Capilano, as my brother Joe and I went to live with her after my father died and my mother was unable to raise all eight of us. I was five or six years old then.

She was a grand lady. She had a nice home in Capilano Creek Reserve and she was quite active. No one ever really knew her age but we think she was born around 1840, which would make her about seventy-seven at the time. I remember, she used to go in her dugout canoe from the Capilano Reserve across the narrows into Vancouver where the old Immigration Building used to be. The Harbour Board used to have a wharf in front of the Immigration Building. That's where my grandmother used to tie up her canoe. There was somebody there all the time so no one could touch her canoe. They had a lot of respect for my grandmother. They used to help her go up the steep ramp when the tide was out. She would have a little buggy with her berries. That was her place to berth her canoe. From Capilano, she would go around Brockton Point, follow the beach all the way around from Prospect Point, then cross when the tide was coming in. The tide would go out in the morning and the tide would come in the evening when she was going home. She knew when to cross, when there was hardly any traffic. She'd tie up there and pack her clams, berries, baskets and mats to the Hotel Vancouver and around the West End where all the rich people lived — the Rogers, MacMillans, McDermids, Bell-Irvings — all those people used to ask my grandmother to bring them fresh berries and clams. She used to keep busy going there about three times a week even if she got only five cents a pound. This was around 1917, so I guess five cents was worth something then. People used to visit her from Mount Currie, Sliammon, Sechelt to trade with her with roots and baskets. She would give them clothes that she got from her sales in Vancouver. She kept this up all her life until she died in 1942. My grandmother was known by many people all through the coast. She could speak five languages — Squamish, Musqueam, Chilcotin, Lillooet and Chinook. I used to sit and listen to them when strangers or white men would come over and start talking Chinook. Chinook jargon, it was a trading language made up from French, English, Cree and other Indian languages. It was used a lot in them days. There's not too many today know Chinook.

Even when she was over a hundred she was trying to cross to Vancouver and wouldn't let anyone stop her. She did capsize one time and she just floated ashore with her canoe. One day she made up her mind she was going to go up where she used to pick blueberries across the Marine Drive bridge over the Capilano River. There was a trail she took up all the way to the suspension bridge. At that time, she lost her direction. She kept wandering around and around. It started to get dark. One thing she remembered was Sisters Creek. She must have followed that creek all the way down to the mouth. The Capilano River was just a little too high. She waded along the shore of Sisters Creek right to Marine Drive where the bridge was; she crawled up. This was about two in the morning. There was no traffic, as Marine Drive was just a two-lane road from West Van to North Van. Auntie Emma, my mother's sister, and I stayed up late that night. We had been out looking for my grandmother. My auntie said, "Let's go out once more and see if we can find her." We went up Capilano Road; it must have been three or four o'clock in the morning. Sure enough, when we got near Marine Drive, we could see her coming. She had a stick. Oh my god! My auntie almost cried. Of course, Grandmother started talking. "Oh, I went there, I got lost," she rambled on. We took her home. I always say there was someone looking after her to be able to walk along that creek in deep water. We took her home and put her to bed. After that she was pretty well bedridden. That was sort of her last effort. It was lucky she didn't die on the river, by drowning. My Auntie Emma was getting after her for going off like that. My grandmother, though over a hundred at the time, still had her eyesight, her hearing, and she even still had good teeth. It was only her body that was getting frail, and her mind wandered at times. She never had rheumatism or any diseases, so she was healthy for her age.

I always had that respect for her. She was more like my mother because she raised me. I called her Ta-ah, which means mother. It can represent grandmother, too.

After that time when she got lost, she was never the same. After work, I used to go over and visit her. Emily, my wife, and I didn't live too far away. She'd be sitting up in her bed. She used to talk a lot about the past. She talked about what I should do, listen to my uncle Chief Mathias Joe, Dominic Charlie. "You go sit and listen, they want to teach you something. We have decided, even though my son, Mathias, is the chief, that you are to be the father of our family. Before my husband died, when your mother was carrying you, he said, 'If it's a boy you take him and train him.'" My grandfather, Joe Capilano, died in November 1910, and I was born in January 1911.

She taught me to bring home the pay cheque, how to take care of the food, how to take care of the family, always respect women because you come from a woman.

It was through her that we had the "Cup of Tea Party" with just a few of us. We would visit house to house. Near my uncle's place was a little field. We sat around talking and laughing and the children played around. "Gee, it was a good idea," Aunt Emma said. So after my grandmother died, we decided that we should get together once in a while. One thing we would do is meet every Good Friday at the cemetery. We would work together to clean it up, then we'd all have a big dinner together, all the families.

Then we started the sports because our children were growing up. We invited a few from North Vancouver and even Vancouver to a sports day where we had tug of war, sack races for everybody. We cleared more land and had a great big space. That's how the Capilano Indian Community Club got started. We had track and field meets and also we started having powwows.

I believe all this was because of my grandmother's teaching, the talking of the elders.

It was a little over a year from the time my grandmother got lost to when she died. It was in the early afternoon. I was working that day and I remember someone saying, "Come and see all those killer whales in the inlet." My grandmother always said she was a member of the whale family. She would go out in the inlet fishing every day to talk to the whales, as they travelled north. In 1942, she was bedridden, all she had left was that her bedroom faced the sea. She called her daughter in and said in Squamish, "Go and greet them, they are coming to say good-bye." Sure enough, her daughter ran down to the beach and saw a whole school of whales coming right into the harbour. When she ran back to tell my grandmother, she was gone; she had died.

We had two nights of wake. Her body was at my uncle Chief Mathias Joe's house. Many people came to have prayers between seven and eight. I stayed all night for two nights even though I had to work during the day. After the wake, she was kept at the undertaker's until she was placed in the tomb with my late grandfather. Everyone that came to respect her said a lot of good things about Mary Capilano for the things she did, people she met; she was honoured by the Queen, honoured by the city. A lot of people came to her funeral to pay their respects.

If it wasn't for my grandmother, Mary Capilano, I wouldn't have the wisdom and knowledge I have today. She would make me sit down and listen when I wanted to get out and play. She was very strong in her traditions, how to survive with nature. I had my chores to do too as a small boy. She would send me out with a wheelbarrow to get wood for us when the tide was out. Every night before she went to sleep she would smoke her pipe. I still remember the smell of the pipe and hearing her strike several matches before she finished.

My grandmother gave two potlatches after my grandfather died. The first one, I'm told, cost her three thousand dollars. I don't know much about this because I was very young. About fifteen years later, around 1925, when I was still at school in Lytton, she gave another memorial potlatch. It wasn't very big. She just called the people to her brother Squamish Jacob's longhouse. She gave people from the Island, Sto:lo Nation and the other Coast Salish people gifts and money. It cost her five or six thousand dollars. In return, they gave her money which was to go to a tomb to be built to house the body of Chief Joe Capilano. A lot of people who respected my grandfather wanted to give him the highest honour, just as is done for the royal family. Others who helped were the Interior Bands and the Nisga'as, the Saanich and even people from Lummi in the United States. My grandmother used the money she had saved up to put on the potlatches and to contribute to building the tomb. I guess you can say the Indians of British Columbia built the tomb to honour my grandfather.

Chief Joe Capilano

My grandfather, Chief Joe Capilano, was known as Hi-Ash Joe. I believe that name was given to him because he was a tall, big man of about six-foot-two or six-foot-three. In Chinook, Hi-Ash means big or huge. That's how he got his name. He was an orphan.

He worked for the government in Fort Langley. He did chores for the government, took canoes out because government officials travelled in canoes them days all the way from Fort Langley to Nanaimo. He was a very good canoeman. He could make canoes and knew how to take care of them.

I believe he learned a lot of things working there. He learned to speak English; he learned a lot of things how the white men do things. That's why years later when he became chief of the Capilanos he had a lot of ideas about trying to get the government to work with the Indians.

I believe he met my grandmother, Mary Agnes, at a reserve that was just the other side of the Patullo Bridge in what is now New Westminster. Fort Langley and New Westminster are not far apart. The reserve just the other side of Patullo Bridge was the first Catholic mission. The four Capilano brothers and their families moved from this area here, Capilano Creek Reserve, to that reserve in what is now New Westminster to be part of the Catholics. Later, when other people began to settle around there, the mission moved to what is now the Catholic Mission Reserve in North Vancouver. My grandmother had married a man from that reserve in New Westminster area, but he had died early of smallpox. She lost all her family.

Hi-Ash Joe met her and they got married. They moved to the Mission Reserve. He got a job as a longshoreman in Moodyville, in what is now part of North Vancouver, where there are great big wheat pools. It was where the sailing ships used to come. My grandfather used to paddle his canoe from the Mission Reserve and walk down a trail to get to Moodyville. Eventually, he became a foreman. He was the first Indian to boss. I remember that some of the old-timers when I went longshoring remembered my grandfather when they worked with the sailing ships. They still knew him as Hi-Ash Joe.

My grandfather was a very devoted Catholic and in them days what money he earned, he gave two-thirds to the church and he kept one-third for themselves. They even built a new church. My grandmother worked with many of the other ladies helping to clear the land. That church is still there today but it has been renovated.

In them days, the church, you might as well say, ran the reserve. They had the most wonderful times there at Christmas and Easter.

Every Christmas Eve, everybody looked forward to midnight mass because we had a good brass band that played on a stage near the back of the church. People would all dress up nice, the children and their parents. Everybody enjoyed the hymns played by the band. There would be a service, a Catholic service. After the service, people would all go home and have a nice big meal with their families. I don't really know when this custom started but it was probably as soon as they had the church.

I always remember when I was older, I played the tuba in the brass band. Everyone looked forward to this time. After the midnight mass, I used to go to my Aunt Molly's. She lived just a few houses from the church. She would put on a big meal. About one-thirty or two in the morning, I'd walk home to my grandmother's in Capilano.

Easter at the Mission Catholic Church was another happy event. They would have all those young people march, like a parade, to the church for confirmation. They wore white gowns. All the parents and children would gather by the road to watch them go to the church, then again, after the service, they would watch as they all went to the school where a big feast was held.

Those were two of the happy occasions of the year at the Catholic Mission.

My Aunt Molly used to tell me about other things that happened in those days. The priests used to go and visit the houses to see if their houses were clean and fences were painted and to check to see if the children were being kept clean or that their hair was combed. Everyone had to obey the nine o'clock curfew.

The priest was in control, and the four Catholic chiefs were the head of the whole Mission Reserve. They were sort of the police. They had a curfew. Anybody got into trouble, the four chiefs would get the person and take them into the Council. They had ways to punish them. Some were made to do community work. Those who didn't want to accept that environment left the community. A lot of them moved to the States.

I don't know how long that lasted, but I know when I came out of school in 1926, things had changed. They had a new priest. The morals of the people changed. They didn't take care of their homes like they did before and the men seemed to be coming home drunk. They seemed to forget how it was before. I used to go there and take my Uncle Peter John home to Mission after payday and I'd see quite a few drunk people around.

I guess in some ways things were better under the control of the church. They had good houses and looked after their families because they all had to be at home by nine o'clock at night. When things changed, with a new priest, it was like the people were free so they did a lot of things that they could not do before, like drinking.

I have been to many healing sessions in the last few years. At those sessions, I hear a lot about the bad treatment by priests and nuns in the villages and the residential schools. People resent the way they were treated like kids with things like a curfew on the reserve and all the abuse that went on in residential schools. I believe the Catholic Church didn't go about it the right way in the early days. There is a lot of feeling of hate about the days when people were controlled by the church and by the school.

Today, we are trying to bring back Indian religions, like the circle healing, smudging. I tell them, "You must practise the principles and the custom of your religion. That's the only way to live. We can't just do something wrong and go and confess and then everything is fine."

It was after the church was built in Mission that they built a school. It was called St. Paul's boarding school. All the children from around Mission went there. Emily, my wife, went there as a day student right up to when she finished grade eight. At the school, they were forbidden, like in a lot of other schools, to speak the Squamish language. They had to learn English and also had to learn lots of Latin words. What good anyone ever did with Latin, I don't know. Latin was used quite a bit in church so they learned how to speak some Latin, but I believe they didn't understand the meaning of the Latin words.

My grandfather and grandmother decided to move from Mission to Capilano Creek Reserve, which was the traditional territory of my grandmother's people. When they moved to Capilano, they had to start all over again. He logged the area. A lot of fine mature timber was taken out to Hastings Mill. The mill was on the west side of the Canadian fish dock where the BC Sugar refinery is. They were given half of the lumber from the timber. The mill kept the other half as payment. They built seven homes on Capilano Reserve with that lumber. My grandmother's uncles and cousins moved there with them.

So all that time, my grandfather started calling the people together to talk about land claims. People came to the longhouse, which was at my uncle Issac Jacob's place. For six or seven months, people came together to talk.

My grandfather, Hi-Ash Joe, was given the name Joe Capilano during the time he was the chief. Just before he was going to England in 1906, the B.C. Indian leaders got together on the

Cambie Street grounds where the old bus depot used to be. He was officially given that Capilano name and a blanket was put on him in a ceremony. He was a well-respected leader. Hi-Ash Joe was not really a Capilano. It was my grandmother who was a Capilano. Her father was one of four brothers who were Capilanos. The brothers had mostly daughters who married and moved away to Comox, Duncan, Musqueam. My grandmother was the daughter of one of them Capilano brothers. She was recognized as one of the leaders and because the people felt the Capilano name was a respected name, they wanted Hi-Ash Joe to have that name. He was to be known as Chief Joe Capilano.

The day came when the Nisga'a, Kwakiutl, Sto:lo, Interior Indians got together. They believed my grandfather because he spoke well. They said, we want to send you to England to talk to the King. One of the old-timers who was related to my grandfather had a whole bunch of cattle. While they were having those meetings, they killed one cow each day to feed the people. Finally, they decided on the delegates to go to England. There were three from the Nisga'a, some from the Sto:lo, Mount Currie. I don't know how many went altogether. They went from here by train. That was in 1906. They had to wait a couple of weeks in Quebec to get on one of those big steam liners. It took them about two or three weeks to sail there. When they got there, they had nobody there to welcome them. They just wanted to get an audience with the King but nobody would have anything to do with them. But during that time, my grandfather met one of the men who used to work for the government in Langley. He shook his hand and said, "Chief, how can I help you?" My grandfather told him what they were there for. The fellow arranged the meeting. That's how they got to see King Edward VII. My grandfather presented his brief to the King in Buckingham Palace. The brief was on land claims, fishing and hunting and on education for the Indian children. My grandfather sang a welcome song to the King, thanking him for his brief:

hi, hi, chi, hup, cháyap, hi, hi,
chi, hi yap, cháyap,
hu-u . . . i, i, i, hi ya.

The song is one of giving thanks to the Great Spirit for all the things you have today and things to come in the future. The King says, "You go back home and we'll send word to your government."

At that time, my grandfather also met the famous Mohawk poet Pauline Johnson. She was there in London to give a recital of her poetry. He was surprised when she came up to him and started speaking Chinook. Later, when she moved to Vancouver, he told her many legends that were published in 1911 as the *Legends of Vancouver*. She was the only English-speaking person that heard the legends from my grandfather.

My grandfather waited for about a year to hear from the government. When he heard nothing he went again, to Ottawa. They gave him a hard time. That's when the government was enforcing new laws on the Indians. Indians were not to fight against the government or they'd be thrown in jail. My grandfather was thrown in jail in Vancouver after he came back. I heard that he went on a hunger strike so they had to let him out. My grandfather struggled to get rights for the Indian people of B.C.

Our Capilano Reserve developed with nice homes. Each home had a tap because that was the agreement the reserve had with North Vancouver. They lived quite well in those days. Some men were longshoring and some were logging. Things got tough sometimes but we never got to the stage where our people went hungry because our people, the Capilanos, had canoes. If you didn't have one, you made one. That's how the people survived. We'd go out and dig clams, fishing. Sometimes the men would go out and shoot ducks which they would share. The same thing when they went deer hunting. When they came home, they'd share their meat with the people. There was no way that anybody was starving. We had fresh and salted salmon, dried salmon, and we'd get a lot of fresh fruit.

When my grandfather died in November 1910, they had those people from other reserves come down from all over B.C. There was just Keith Road then, no Marine Drive. They carried his body all the way up Keith Road, and he was buried in the Capilano cemetery, which is still used by us today.

My uncle Mathias Joe became the chief after my grandfather died. There was a lot of controversy over the Capilano name, so he didn't use it except once in a while when he was referred to as Chief Mathias Joe Capilano. Some of the descendants of the four Capilano brothers are to this day wanting to reclaim the Capilano name. So, it seemed better not to use the name any more for the descendants of Hi-Ash Joe, Chief Joe Capilano.

My uncle Mathias Joe was a real good leader. I learned a lot of things from him as a promoter. The people from outside really respected him. Whenever there was something going on, he was the leader, him and Andy Paull. A lot of times, he was the co-ordinator of celebrations going on. He was a great speaker. When I was a little boy, I travelled with him to Indian Days. My uncle was always the leader co-ordinating in North Vancouver and Vancouver. He was respected on and off the reserve. He was on the Council. He automatically became a councillor after amalgamation when the sixteen Squamish reserves got together. He explained to them that with amalgamation, we had to work together, to share things. I think at that time, Capilano had gravel and the most land to develop.

He got a lot of recognition from the city, from the government. He went to England twice, he went to Queen Elizabeth's coronation. He and his wife were the first to cast their votes when the federal vote came in in 1960. He was a good hard-working man, a longshoreman and a leader of his people. Like many people, even today, if alcohol gets a hold of you, it does cause problems. He had some problems, but all the same he helped his people.

They wanted me to take his place on the hereditary line after he died to carry on the work that he was doing. I didn't take the chieftainship, but I did carry on the work and I am the father of the Capilano family. That's what my grandfather and grandmother wanted.

My grandmother, Mary Capilano, circa 1935

Mary Capilano with Lizzie Joseph (*left*) and Rose (Posie) Mathias (*centre*), circa 1939

My grandfather, Chief Joe Capilano (*front, fourth from left*), with delegation leaving for Ottawa in 1906

Funeral procession for Chief Joe Capilano, 1910

My uncle, Chief Mathias Joe, with Coast Salish ceremonial headdress

My mother, Susan Baker, daughter of Joe and Mary Capilano

Chief Mathias Joe on his way to London for the coronation of Elizabeth II in 1953, carrying gifts for the queen (Bill Dennett/ *Vancouver Sun*)

My Paternal Grandparents

My Aunt Emma told me about our Baker grand-parents. She told me that my grandfather, John Baker, was an Englishman who used to come on the sailing ships. My grandmother, Mary Tsiyaliya, a tall charming young Squamish woman, who looked like she had white blood, met John Baker. They got married. He built a hotel in Gastown. He was well-to-do, but the hotel burned down and he lost everything.

They had two sons and four daughters. My dad was the oldest son, so he was called John Baker. They called him Johnny Baker most of the time. His brother was Willie and the girls were Charlotte, Molly, Lizzie and Nora. When my grandfather died, they were living on Deadman's Island, the little island where the navy is near Stanley Park. He was buried there. After he died the Indian people invited my grandmother, Mary Tsiyaliya Baker, to return to the Mission Reserve. They had already built the Catholic church. When they brought them over they had to join the church. My grandmother and her teen-aged daughters were told they all had to marry Indians from around there.

Those days, the church didn't want to have a half-breed marrying a half-breed, so they all married Indians from the reserve. My grandmother married Squamish Jacob. The oldest girl, Lizzie, married Chief Joseph, who was the chief of the Mission Reserve. Charlotte, the second oldest girl, married Jake Lewis, who originally came from Kitsilano. The third one was Molly. She married George Band. The Band name was given to him because he was the leader of a brass band at the time. The last one, Nora, who was the darkest one, very pretty, married Napoleon Moody. Willie married Mary Ann, Squamish Jim's daughter. My dad married my mother, Susan.

My Parents and Brothers and Sisters

When my dad married my mother, he was around thirty years old and she was only fifteen. It was his second marriage.

I didn't really know my dad because when he died in 1915 I was quite young, only four years old. My oldest brother, Bill, told me about our dad. He said he was a fisherman, a very good worker. He built gill net boats and he was hired as a net boss at one of the canneries. A net boss is the one who looks after all the net gear. He had to know how to handle the fishermen. Those canneries were quite large so he had quite a job.

One of the canneries was around Rivers Inlet. All of the family would go with my father when he went there to work. My brother said there were a lot of knotholes in the wharf. I guess I used to look through these knotholes at the little fish. Whenever I wasn't around our place, they knew where I would be. One time they came and found me there sleeping with my eye pressed against a knothole.

After my father died, my brother Bill got one of the gill net boats my father built. He used the boat to go fishing to look after us. In June, Bill got married and moved away, but our family still had the use of the boat. Sometimes we'd go beachcombing.

I was told my dad was the coach of the first Indian lacrosse team we had. My grandfather, Joe Capilano, was the manager, that was when my uncle Mathias Joe and Willie Baker were players.

My dad joined the brass band and played the clarinet. He was a big tall man. They say I resemble him quite a bit.

He died of pneumonia. All I can remember about his death was hearing men hammering. I didn't know what they were doing but I guess they were building his coffin. Then what stuck in my mind was seeing him in this box with one lit candle on top of the coffin. That candle stuck in my mind for many years. He wasn't very old when he died. He had been logging just before that in very bad weather. He was a good provider. If he had lived I believe we could have been well off.

My mother, Susan, was the daughter of Joe and Mary Capilano. She was a very strong woman. She held on to our Indian culture. She went to school for only one or two years. She was a big girl for her age. My grandmother took her out of the boarding school because she couldn't speak English and they would punish her all the time for speaking Squamish. She could only learn to write her name and a few words. Later on she learned to speak good English. She learned it from outside when she married my dad, who was a half-breed. My mother knew everything about our ways, our culture. She knew how to prepare our food, dried salmon, everything. She also made baskets of all kinds. Before brother Bill was born she made a basket that she used to put him in. She hung the basket somehow from a split maple. She would tie a string to her toe and make the basket go up and down. That way she could keep working with her hands, making baskets or knitting. The basket of cedar and cedar roots was so strong she used it for all of us eight children.

My mother had seven boys and one girl. All of us were born at home. My brothers were Bill, Bobby, Charlie, Joe, Jim and Dan. Charlie died when he was only twelve years old. I always remember that after my dad died, Charlie had to look after us younger kids when my mother went housekeeping in Vancouver. Those were hard times. That's why Joe and I were sent to live with my grandmother, Mary Capilano. My brother Jim died of spinal meningitis at boarding school.

Irene was our only full sister. She was born after my dad died.

My mother later married Billy Snow. She had three children with him. The oldest girl, Elizabeth, died of third-degree burns in a fishing boat. The boy only lived for two years. The only sister left is Amy, who married a man from Cape Mudge. She had nineteen children. Only nine are living today.

So, of all my brothers and sisters from the two families of my mother, only Amy, Irene and I are living. Emily and I visit Amy in Campbell River once in a while, and she and her family come here to visit sometimes. My sister Irene lives in Capilano. She was married and lived in Yakima, Washington, and Seattle for many years. When she was younger, she worked as a nurse. She wasn't trained but she was very good at it.

Irene and I talk on the phone almost every day when we are not visiting each other. Sometimes if I don't call her during the day, she'll call me and say, "What's the matter, brother, have you got a broken arm?" We have a lot of fun, but she's been quite sick lately. I worry about her.

The other day, I was telling her about our late brother Joe. I told her that brother Joe had very good eyes. We were all taught range shooting at school. We used big rifles. In a national competition, he got a medal. He came second. A Six Nations man came first. That medal of my brother's stayed in that school at Lytton. Joe was also a pool shark and a great ping-pong player.

Boyhood Recollections: In Them Days . . .

It's kind of hard to remember back about eighty years, what it was like here in Capilano. I know there have been many changes, like Marine Drive. When I was a boy, it was just a wagon road.

There were about seven families living in Capilano, all relatives of my grandmother, uncles and cousins in them days. The houses were not far apart, sort of like today. My dad built our house before he died. The houses were small, mostly they had two big rooms. One was a kitchen where we ate. The other room, we had beds. I remember that in our house, there was only one big bed that my mother and dad slept on. Us kids all slept on the floor. My grandmother's house was about the same. I never thought anything about our house being small. That's how it was for everybody.

I remember there was a pipeline along Capilano Road. The pipeline used to service the water for the city. There was only one road and the Pacific Great Eastern railway. People would ride on the train to Horseshoe Bay. The train went by close to where we lived. We used to watch the train and all the people sitting in an outdoor observation car in the summertime.

We liked going over to play at Walter Neuman's place. He was the caretaker of the pipeline. He lived in a beautiful home down the beach. There was a big platform outside his place covering the pipes. I remember that we had a lot of fun playing on that platform. He had quite a few kids. Walter Neuman was not an Indian but his kids all learned to speak Squamish because they always played with my brothers and me. All we spoke was Squamish in them days.

Not far from us, there was Japanese people living. They had two or three houses. I played with these Japanese boys, but during the war they took them away.

It was nothing for us to walk all the way to the streetcar line. There were three streetcars. One went straight up Lonsdale, the other to Lynn Valley and the third to Capilano, at the present upper levels. The Capilano line ended where they had a post office and a store where our families used to go to do our shopping.

There was a theatre at North Vancouver city, the Empire Theatre, on what is now First Street and Lonsdale. We used to go on the streetcar. Sometimes we had no money but they'd let us on anyway. Most of the time we'd walk. For us young boys, it was nothing to walk it.

We always liked to go to the movie theatre. There were mostly westerns like Buck Jones, Tom Mix. It cost five cents to go in the show. Sometimes I didn't have any money and I'd go and stand in front of the theatre and someone would pity me and give me five cents so I could go in.

There was always something for us boys to do. In the summer, we were nearly always at the beach. We spent a lot of time swimming. I learned to swim when I was only five years old. My brother Bill pushed me off the canoe that time and I had to learn to swim, at least to dog-paddle. We used to like watching the older boys diving. Once I knew how to swim, no one could keep me away from the water. We could dive like a rock and swim like a fish. We even used to swim during high tide right across to Lumbermen's Arch. I only did it once but the Jacob boys and the Johnson boys, they could go back and forth. There wasn't much traffic on the narrows in them days.

There was always something to do; we were never lonesome. Sometimes, we'd pick clams to take home or we would tie up good-looking logs, cedar, cut them up for wood.

I remember when we'd take a canoe up Capilano River to the West Vancouver slough to go fishing. We used to go up that slough, way up to where them three towers are today on the north side of Park Royal. There was quite a stream there. We could catch trout, dog salmon or coho, mostly coho.

I guess, somehow, we were natural carvers. I can remember as a small boy getting old shingles and carving paddles out of them.

The eight years I spent in school, 1918 to 1926, I only came home for one month in the summer. Every year that I'd come home there was something different, more buildings, more roads, some paved.

2

SCHOOL DAYS, SCHOOL DAYS

Leaving Home

I can always remember the first time I left home. My grandmother was busy making clothes. She didn't go to the store to buy ready-made clothing; she got clothing in exchange for her baskets. She'd get half clothes and half money from her baskets. A lot of the men's clothes she'd cut up and make me pants that would go to my knees, like short pants. I would then wear stockings and have to tie them with rags to keep them up because she didn't have garters for me. She'd make shirts and she'd somehow have used jackets that sort of fit.

One day she got me all dressed up and I wondered why. We would get dressed up for special occasions like going to big Indian Days. My grandmother used to dress me up and we'd row across in a canoe to Stanley Park. It was not far, just on the east side of Lumbermen's Arch. That was the only time we dressed up until this time. I thought, "I guess we're going to go to some celebration." I got all ready with a bag with a little clothing in it. She said, "Well, we're going to send you to school." I was just seven years old and when I heard school, I thought, "Well, it's not going to be too far." My uncle, Chief Mathias, had two of his daughters that were going, too. There were three of us, my brother Joe, he was older, my brother Jim, who was younger than I am, and me. My brother Dan was too young to go yet. So instead of going to North Vancouver to catch the ferry, we went all the way to Vancouver where she used to tie her canoe, at the foot of Granville Street. That was right close to the CPR station. Away we went, into the big building to board the train. My uncle, Chief Mathias, came with us, and his wife, Ellen, because they had two of their daughters going. We left at nine o'clock in the morning and we got to Lytton at three o'clock in the afternoon, in August. So you can imagine that it was quite hot, and there was a breeze blowing. It felt like a breeze out of an oven. So we waited there and finally a horse and buggy arrived to meet us. All of us crowded in there. It was more like a wagon than anything else. It was about three miles from the Lytton station across the Thompson River bridge and up a hill to where the residential school was. We got there early. We were the first ones to arrive. I can always remember seeing this great big building. I couldn't figure it out. We all felt a bit excited. We were taken into the building and shown around. So we were all taken downstairs and they gave us school clothing. They took our own clothes and put them away and that was the last time we saw our clothes. They gave us socks, shoes, shirts, pants and bedding. We were told where to sleep in the big dormitory.

We were not used to sleeping in beds. So my brother Joe said, "Let's throw our mattresses on the floor." So we did, and we got into bed, clothes and all. We didn't put on the nightgowns we were given. The principal and my uncle came in to wake us up the next morning, and at first glance, they couldn't see us. We were not on the beds. Then they saw us all sleeping on the floor under the beds. My uncle just laughed and told the principal that was how we slept at home. "It will take them time to get used to sleeping on a high bed," he explained.

My uncle and my aunt stayed overnight and left the next day. Anyway, the day they left was one of the most sorrowful days of my life. I was so close to my uncle, and having them leave us there, it was sad, I couldn't understand what was happening. My older brother Joe seemed to take control then and told us we had to listen, that this is where we were going to be for the year until we go home for holiday.

The next three or four days, there were children coming in from everywhere. They were coming in buggies, wagons, and some were walking. The first thing we knew, we had forty some-odd boys, maybe more, and about the same number of girls arrived. We soon realized we had to get accustomed to the rules of the school. You had to learn to obey, making your bed, having your bath, going to your regular meals, you had to wash your hands. We had to say our grace and pray in the morning, and in the evening. We knew we had to do our chores, such as sweeping the dormitory, cleaning the washrooms, in the morning, and go to school half a day. We had our chores to do in the afternoon. Then we had our supper, but after supper was play time. We played around until bedtime. That was the regular routine of that school.

I was just learning how to speak English, and getting acquainted with all the children who had different languages from different tribes took some time to get used to.

We hardly ever saw our two cousins there, Chief Mathias Joe's daughters; we only saw them in the schoolroom or at mealtimes because we all ate in the same dining room. The girls sat on one side and the boys on the other. We had a big playground and we would talk to the girls from far away by hollering so they could hear us. We would try to see how they were doing. As time went by, we didn't have to talk to them because we got to know other children. Because we were young, we stuck more with the boys, playing together, and didn't think much about the girls.

We had to get used to the school rules. I guess we were satisfied to have a bed, a place to eat, a place for recreation, a field outside to play in.

I've Got to Learn

Every year as we grew older, we got heavier duties to do, such as working on the farm. There was a big farm with dairy cattle, pigs, chickens, working horses. I can remember the first time I was to milk the cows. I was a beginner. I was so anxious about this. I was told to go to the end and start there. So as usual, I did as I was told. I got down to the end and thought, "Gee, this is a funny-looking cow." The guys were all watching me. I went to the cow and the damn thing almost kicked me out. Here it was a bull. The boys had their joke and the next time I knew. We had two cows each to milk in the morning and in the evening. We had to get up at six in the morning, did all our milking, went back to the school and had breakfast and then we had other chores to do, like feeding the pigs, cleaning the barn, churning the milk to make butter. We would put it in a big container to separate the fat, cream, out of the milk. We drank a lot of the buttermilk. This part I really enjoyed. When we got to our table we seldom got butter and I wondered why, but later I realized that all the butter was being sold. They sold the vegetables, apples. From these sales our clothing was provided. So we really worked year after year. Our job was getting tougher. We went to school for half a day. One month you worked in the mornings and the next month you worked in the afternoons. We never went to school full-time until the last year, in grade eight.

We didn't really get into the education until we were around grade three. Before, we were just drawing, learning A, B, C. Later on we learned our addition, how to add, and geography and history. When we got into about grade four or five, we had to get into literature. We had to read books and write stories. It was quite difficult at times, but with most of the teachers we had, not at any time that I can remember were they mean to us. Of course, we always had a few kids who were kind of backward, but they were never punished, they were just given extra work. Sometimes we used to help the ones who needed it. I always had that in my mind because I was brought up by my people, the teaching I got was to always try to help the other person. I guess that's why I recognize a lot of them today; I used to take the lower class out who were having problems, go for a walk. I believe I learned a lot just by trying to teach others the right way of thinking, to try to keep out of trouble. My own personal thinking has always been, "I've got to learn, I've got to do this for the rest of my days."

I taught them about nature, making a bow and arrow, little canoes, to get their minds off problems. I also got them to play sports. I was good at it and I encouraged them to play well. We had a good basketball team and a good ball team. It was just the leadership. This helped me later in being a leader. People always called on me to do things and I never hesitated. If they didn't call me, I just went ahead anyway. I didn't believe in being idle. I was always very interested.

When I was young, I sometimes got beat up by the older boys for something they said I did wrong. I never knew what that was most of the time. I never gave up, though, because my brother Joe used to help me out. We really learned to look after ourselves. We were very good in sports, basketball, baseball. My brother Joe was a very good athlete. Everything we did, we seemed to be ahead of the other guys up there. I guess it was just our way. We seemed to know how to do things and the others came to rely on us. That's how we got along out there — very good with the Interior bunch. They came from

Vernon, Lillooet, Boston Bar, Merritt. There were quite a few good boys, clever, very active. They never wanted to hurt anybody. They seemed to want to listen, to learn or to help us, because up there they were farmers, cowboys, and us from the coast were called the canoe builders. We knew how to swim. Many of them didn't know how to swim. We really surprised them in the summertime when we went down to the Fraser River. We'd strip right down and dive right in and swim. Later on we made a dam up by the school. There was a stream there and we made a swimming pool. This is where we taught many of the boys how to swim.

Running Away from School

The first time I ran away from school was when I was thirteen years old. We arrived one week earlier than the other students. There were five of us from the coast: Wilfred Williams, brothers Joe, Henry, Dan, and myself. We were doing all the work, milking the cows, cleaning the barns. One of the boys went up to the loft to pitch the hay down for the cows. The guy, instead of going outside to pee, peed upstairs in the loft, and it leaked right on Mr. Timmins as he walked into the barn. Mr. Timmins was the head of the dairy farm. He questioned all of us until finally Wilfred admitted that he was the guilty one. He got a very bad beating. We couldn't believe that a person could do that. We couldn't do anything but just stand and watch Mr. Timmins hit Wilfred with a great big leather strap that he used to tie the cows' legs. He would strap the legs of cows who were a bit wild when he milked them. That's what he used. So my god, nobody was at the school but us, so we decided to leave. Away we went! We left the school at night, walked down to Lytton, which was three miles away, to the CNR station. It was at about two or three o'clock in the morning when a freight train came along. So we jumped on the locomotive. We travelled all the way down to Port Mann where all the trains stopped. When we got off we couldn't believe how we looked. We were covered with soot that came off the locomotive. We all looked so funny. We laughed at each other. Then we all went down to the riverbank to wash ourselves. We walked from Port Mann all the way home to Vancouver.

We had just enough money to buy one ferry ticket to get to North Vancouver. They said, "Si, you go." So I did, and I walked home from the ferry. I went to see my grandmother. She was shocked to see me as I had been gone for only four days. I explained what happened at the school. She didn't say anything. She didn't try to send me back.

The other boys finally got back as they had to walk a long way around. We stayed at home only one night. My grandmother knew we should not stay around as someone would probably be looking for us, to send us back. She told me where brother Bill had a white man's war canoe hidden in the bush near the beach, near where he had found it. We got blankets and food. We told my grannie that we were going to go up to Squamish. Away we went. We paddled as far as Point Atkinson before dark. We couldn't get around because it was too rough. So we pulled our canoe on the beach. There weren't too many people living in that Whytecliff area at that time. We pulled our canoe up and turned it upside down. The tide was up and we went to sleep. It was raining. When we woke up, the tide was out. We had to drag our canoe a long way to the water. It took us all day to reach Squamish from Point Atkinson.

We were gone for about two weeks. Then one day an Indian policeman arrived in a gas boat. He told us we had to go back to the school. We didn't like to go back, but we had to. Soon we were back on the train heading for Lytton. That was one time that we ran away because one of our boys got beat up so badly. Maybe he did a naughty thing, but he never should have gotten a licking like that.

We ran away another time. We got on a passenger train. We told the conductor, "Oh, we forgot our tickets." He knew we didn't but he let us on the train anyway and took us as far as Boston Bar. From there on we hitchhiked and thought we would get picked up, but we kept walking. We walked a long way. We got very hungry and were so hungry that we went to where they used to dump food off the train. There we found cantaloupe and dried toast. We ate that. When we got right down to Yale, the boys said to me, "I know there are Indians living down that way by the river." The boys asked me to go see if I could get any food. So I went over there and told the people I was hungry. They asked me to come in and fed me roast sockeye and apple pie. I didn't tell them there were others out there. But I told them I'd like a little bit of bread to take with me. So they gave me the bread and I had a great dinner. When I got back to the guys, I told them what I had eaten. I said, "See, you didn't want to come with me so you missed out. All you'll have is a little bit of bread." We made it back home. In a little while, the policeman, the same one, came along to take us back again. So that was twice we ran away from school. They didn't punish us, but they made us obey more rules.

I ran away with another guy one time. His name was Pat Kelly. His dad worked on the PGE, the Pacific Great Eastern. He worked from Lillooet to Squamish. Pat said, "Come on, we'll go." So we went. It was quite a walk from the school to Lillooet, over thirty miles, so we had to sleep out in the open one night. We were sleeping and I woke up suddenly to see a great big lizard coming toward us, so we climbed up a tree. We decided to stay up in the tree all night. I don't know how we kept from falling off. I went another few miles and I said to myself, "I don't like this, going through this hot country with no place to hide on that highway." So we walked all the way back again to school. They seemed to welcome us back again. We never got punished. Anyway, I made up my mind that I wouldn't run away again, it was too tough.

When you live a hundred and sixty miles from home, it's very hard to try to get home. We wondered how we never got hurt or killed or got poisoned eating that discarded food.

We Work Like Men So We Eat Like Men!

All those years I was in school, I was always sort of a leader. If anything was to be organized, they would always say, "Let's get Simon, he'll be the head of it." That's how I happened to organize a strike at the age of fourteen, at Lytton Residential School. The older boys were expected to do heavy work, and we did not feel like we were getting enough to eat so we could do these jobs. In other words, we were hungry! We wondered what we could do about this. There didn't seem to be any rights for the students. We certainly had no part in any decision-making. We were just told what to do all the time. In fact, we had to answer to bells all the time like well-trained rats. A bell would ring to wake us, another bell for chores, bell for meals, for chapel, for school, for study time, for bedtime. I still think I should jump up and do something when I hear bells even after nearly seventy years away from it.

We had to do something about the hunger situation; we had let it go on long enough. As we did our chores, we tried to think of what to do. I knew something about strikes and I told the boys that we'd go on strike. We were all a bit afraid to take a chance. We could have our heads shaved or get strapped or lose our privileges. Privileges were few, so that was no real threat. I told the boys, "The only way it will work is if we are sure to stick together, all of us, with no one backing down."

They wouldn't expel all of us, we thought, nor would they dare severely punish all of us.

Well, the boys agreed. We would all go to the principal, Mr. Lett. Bravely one morning, before heading out to do our chores, we marched to the principal's office. I was delegated to be the spokesman. The issue was, we work like men so we should eat like men, so you better give us more food on our table. I said, "If we don't get it, we'll steal, go into the kitchen and steal a loaf of bread or something like that." Mr. Lett just stared at me and said, "You're quite honest." I said, "Yeah, either we get it or we're going to take it." That was one of the things I'll always remember that my grandmother taught me. If you want something, go and ask. To our surprise the principal did not oppose us. Instead, our demand was met, but I always felt he had it against me for promoting the idea of a strike.

That taught me a lesson about leadership, about going after what you want, changing conditions for the better. I guess, in a way, it was good that we went hungry because it forced me to organize a way out of it.

Posing for the camera at age fourteen

At school, age fifteen

With Bill Walkum (*left*), and Kenny Walkem (*right*) while we were away at school

Me with friends Walter Bent (*left*) and Peter Maneebaret (*centre*)

The Only Thing That Changed Is We Grew Older

Year after year went by at the boarding school and the only thing that changed is that we grew older. Some of the children grow up and leave and you always have newcomers. I would go home for one month each year, in July. Even then, I would seldom see my grandmother, because she'd get up early to pick berries or dig clams and get home quite late in the evening. The month didn't seem very long.

Somehow I was always glad to go back to school, to the routine that I had gotten used to. I knew I had to try to learn things. Staying home at my age when I was thirteen or fourteen was very difficult. It was the time of the Depression and people were really struggling to feed themselves. Being in school meant you had a bed, three meals a day, you went to church in the morning and in the evening. For recreation, we did a lot of things. I promoted a lot of games, games I learned as I watched the older boys at home before I went to school. One was called stink hole. It was a game that we learned from our older brothers. It was a game similar to cricket. We used to dig a hole, and that hole was the base where you stood and you hit the ball. When you hit that ball you gotta run a certain distance and get back before the guy gets the ball and throws it to the catcher. If he gets the ball ahead and puts it in the hole, you were out. Sometimes we played it all day long. We just take turns, like in a circle. The guy catching will bat and the guy that was pitching will catch, and it just keeps going around and around like that. It took a little while before some of the boys caught on to it. Once they got into it, they really seemed to enjoy it. Everybody tried so hard to get as many runs as possible. Whoever got the most runs was the champ. It was quite an enjoyable game.

Duck in a rock was another game we played. It was similar to the stink hole game. You put one rock on top of another rock, and you try to knock the top rock off. If you hit that rock quite a ways, you have to run to a certain distance and back. It's quite interesting because you got to get a round rock, about a little bigger than a ball, and the one that you have on top is a little smaller. You have to be a good pitcher to be able to hit it. And if you miss, well, you lose.

Another game we used to play was auntie high over. This game could be played in teams. We played it at the barn, which had quite a roof. One team would throw the ball over the roof and holler, "Auntie high over." The other team would catch the ball and everyone on that team would run around the barn. The team that threw it would try not to get caught as *they* ran around the barn. The team doing the chasing could throw the ball at the players. If it hit anyone, that guy would have to join the other team. Running around the big barn meant we had to step over manure pies. Sometimes one of the guys would slip and he would be quite a mess. So we were always doing something. We made our own fun.

The children liked to learn the games. They caught on well! Later on, I got into making things. I made bows and arrows. We used to put chicken feathers on the end. We even found quite a few arrowheads. We found these near the mouth of the Thompson and Fraser rivers. There was kind of a bar there, a sandhill. We would go there on Saturdays and dig. The arrowheads were made out of flintstone. Some were long ones; some were short. They were really professionally made. We didn't use those arrowheads on our bows. We'd use nails and go hunting rabbits, squirrels and chipmunks. Jack pine trees were common in that area. Sometimes we'd shoot a squirrel fifteen feet up and it would stick to the jack pine. Then we would have a hard time to get it down. We'd skin them, dry them, then use them for decoration on our hats or jackets.

I started carving. I carved a fourteen-inch replica of a fifty-foot canoe with all the seats and paddles. I was surprised that I could do it. I'd seen these kinds of boats every year at the festivals. We had about four in North Vancouver. I'd go and watch them build these canoes. I used to watch old man Julian and old man Harry Moody when they were making their last canoe that they made for our North Shore Indians. They'd start with a fifty-foot log and carve it. When they were finished you wouldn't think it was a log because it was beautifully carved and could travel quite fast.

The senior teacher at that time was Mr. Anfield. He took a great interest in whatever I did. He always seemed to help me, encourage me. So I presented him with that canoe, and you know, when he died, his wife and son asked me to be a pall-bearer. I went to the house after the funeral and I saw that he still had that canoe. This would be thirty some-odd years later. That is something I always say, the Indian has talent.

After I started carving at school, the other boys began to carve. They made whistles and other things from that wood. I remember those trips to the woods, especially at berry-picking time. There were saskatoon and soap berries used to make Indian ice cream, *sxwúsum*. We picked them when they were still green and they made good white ice cream, but when they were ripe, they were like currants. Many kinds of berries grow in that Lytton, Thompson area. The people there had their ways of getting their food. I used to watch them dip net, catch sockeye and sun-dry it. They just hang them up, and heat from the rock blown by a breeze would be like heat from an oven. They'd dry it just perfect so they could keep it all winter. They would cut the fish in squares because it cured better that way. I always enjoyed eating the wind-dried fish whenever I had a chance. Today, I even buy it, if someone has some from the Interior.

We were always active, always doing something when we weren't doing our chores. In the evening after supper, especially during my last two years there, I did a lot of reading, studying. I didn't play as much then.

After I left school, I kept on reading. Something seemed to tell me that you have to advance your knowledge, you have to advance your education.

I liked reading the newspaper, especially the sports section. I was sports-minded in every way, like boxing, baseball, football and lacrosse. Lacrosse was a big thing in them days, not only here in Vancouver, but all across the country. The Mohawks of St. Regis in Ontario were often in the news. I followed the world's best boxers: Jack Johnson, Georges Carpentier and others. When I went to L.A. in later years, I went to Disneyland, where there is a great big building with information just about boxing. I spent three hours there, reading the whole time.

Anything to do with sports, I really liked. I was always good in sports, especially lacrosse and boxing. I was one of the champion players of the famous North Shore Indians. I boxed several rounds in my day and won, too.

So I read about sports in newspapers and whatever magazines I could get hold of. When I graduated, the teacher told me to read as much as possible. "It doesn't matter what you read, read everything; that will keep your mind active," he told me.

Being a Leader

I believe I developed leadership during the time that I lived with my grandmother. She used to leave me at home when she went out, and being home by myself, I guess there's a lot of things that I had to do, like I had to go and get my own food, or try and cook. I started to cook quite early because I used to watch my grandmother, and you had to do things. I did it. I didn't seem to have any problem. It just comes natural. I think that all comes from my grandmother telling me that I got to do things for myself. So in school, when I was young, I used to like to keep the place clean and make sure that there was nothing out of order. The other boys would be just sitting around, and I'd ask them to come and help, or do something. When I woke up in the morning, I knew that day that I had to start the routine, which is that I had to dress myself first, and make sure I'd got my shoes all laced up. I'd always make sure that I was dressed neatly. If there was a button missing, I knew I had to go to the place where they have the needle and buttons, and I'd go sew it on. If my shoelace came off and broke, I made sure if I didn't get a shoelace from school, I managed to get something else to replace it. I never neglected anything that I felt that I could do, unless I was sick or something. That's why when I go out to play with the boys, you know a lot of them would be sitting around, and I used to call them, "Come on in."

Eventually they'd find that it was a lot of fun to play baseball or some other games that we were learning from our older brothers from back home. It got them interested. Nobody taught me to be a leader, but as I said, I was taught by my grandmother, by her ways. I guess that's what created in my mind that I listened, and I find out that listening does a lot of things for me.

I guess I can say I was always a leader at school. During the last two years, I was a prefect or something. I was always at the head of the table. If anything had to be said, I did the talking. I was the leader of the sports, the captain. We travelled to different schools to compete in baseball and basketball. We had a good ball team. I remember Sam Henry, who was a great pitcher. He read everything he could on pitching. He was one of the boys that died of TB. It really hurt us to see him go.

Brother Jim Dies at School

My brother Jim died at the school. He was about thirteen years old. He had spinal meningitis. I remember clearly that there was a new building put up for the older boys. When my brother Jim got very sick he was put in this building to be with me. Jim had bad headaches. I used to hear him crying at night. I asked the principal to take him to the hospital. He didn't. After about two weeks, my brother was in so much pain, he was going out of his mind. I pleaded with the principal for days to take him to a doctor. "For god's sake, you better do something for my brother." They finally took him to the small hospital in Lytton. Each day I would ask how he was doing and they'd say he's doing all right. On the third day, on a Sunday night, the principal's wife came in, spoke to her husband and they called me into the office. There they told me that my brother had just passed away. I went to the hospital with the principal. There lay my brother Jim in a room that was like a morgue.

A coffin was ordered from Kamloops, and the next day the principal told me I had to go with him to put my brother in the coffin.

I used to be afraid of dead people. I always had that fear. You know, when I went down there and seen my brother, we washed him and put some clothing on him, but the coffin was too short, and that's the thing that I couldn't believe, that they wouldn't order another coffin. He had been dead for twenty-four hours, so we had to break his knees to put him in his coffin. It was hot out, so the body had started to smell. When I got back to the school, I could smell that odour. It stayed with me for a while. From then on, I wasn't afraid of dead people. I guess my brother did take that fear from me, by handling him myself. We phoned my grandmother to tell her of Jim's death. So she came up to go back by train to North Vancouver with the body. I went with her. We took the body to the undertaker in North Vancouver. My grandmother said to them, "You order a new coffin so I can put my grandson in a good one." We buried my brother in the Squamish cemetery in North Vancouver.

When I got home here the Shakers people were quite strong, she made me go to the Shakers that night. She believed in the power of the Shakers people. They were to take away my fear of the dead. They pray first in their language. Then Isaac, he was the head, put out the candles, and then they start. And then they all start to move around, they seem to touch one another, I guess to get the power working together. Then the first one comes and grabs me on the head, and the next one comes and touches my arm, and so on. Oh, it's just like it goes right through you. The last one I guess got up and started to sing loud, jump and ring the bell. When they opened the door, I guess that is when whatever it is is supposed to go out. Then they start praying, praying, praying. So I had to sit there. When we were all finished, then they come and they shake my hand. They went through me, they seemed to take whatever it was, threw it out. When I finished, it was like I was cleaned and I wasn't afraid. I went back to school and I just couldn't seem to believe what had happened because I had always been a coward of the dead.

It was hard going back to school in Lytton. I got so close to my brother during those days when he was sick. A lot of things were in my mind as I travelled back on the train. Jim was a really good athlete, a nice-looking boy. I guess you could say he was a daredevil. Him and Henry Jacobs used to do things you wouldn't believe. They rode bucking horses and they used to jump on pigs in the pigpen. They did a lot of crazy things. I think maybe that is how he got injured and got meningitis. He seemed to be very healthy and lively until he suddenly got sick.

All this happened during my last year at school, the year I was finishing my grade eight. I was fifteen, just two years older than Jim. I knew there was nothing to stay home for and I wanted to be with the boys at the school, my bed and the three meals a day that I was used to.

Going Home

I was looking forward to leaving school but I wasn't sure what I would do at home. I hoped I could go on and further my education.

I remember that last day of school. There were five of us that stuck close together. There were the two Walkem boys, Kenneth and Bill, and Antoine Peters and his sister Janet. They were all from the Lytton area, so I knew I wouldn't be seeing them very much. We did keep in touch, though. Only Bill is living today.

I guess it was even harder to leave the girl I had a crush on. She was smart and kind of short. Her name was Margaret McIntyre. She stuck with me all that afternoon until it was time for me to catch my train. I remember telling her that someday I'd come back.

I was glad to be back at home with my grandmother after being away at boarding school for eight years. It seemed an exciting time to be on the Capilano Reserve down by the First Narrows. I loved to watch the big ships coming in, both passenger ships and old Union Steamships. There would be a stream of them leaving from 8:30 A.M. and begin returning by 3:30 P.M., with the last one arriving around 11:00 P.M. The ships always blew their whistles going out and coming in.

During that time, I helped my grandmother as much as I could. There was a lot of wood that would drift into the slough near where we lived. I used to go in the canoe and gather up all the lumber. If it was a big log, I would tow it in and cut it up for firewood or cut it up for cedar shakes. I was kept busy during that year that I stayed with my grandmother.

Finally, I decided that if I was going to further my education, I had better start seriously planning for it. One day, I approached my grandmother, who by then was in her nineties, about my plans. I told her I wanted to go to the white man's school to further my education. She sat there for quite a few minutes, not saying a word. I kept looking at her and wondering why she wasn't speaking. Finally I asked her, "What's the matter, Ta-ah? Is there something wrong? Did I say something wrong?" She continued her silence a while longer. Finally she said, "Son, I don't want you to go to white man's school because I have been teaching you our way of living and I want you to be the leader of our family here on the Capilano Reserve." I told her that in order to be a leader, I had to have more education, so I could understand and talk like the white man so I could get things for our people. She just sat there and never said a word. I knew that meant she didn't want me to go to white man's school. Hurt and a bit angry, I left the house to think. I decided not to go against my grandmother's wishes, but I did leave home. I went to Yakima, Washington, with my brother Bill.

3

OUT INTO THE WORLD

My First Jobs

My brother Bill was home the year I finished school. He didn't go fishing. He asked me, "How about coming down with me to Yakima, picking hops?" A lot of Indians used to go down there from Vancouver Island and all over, as there were four big hop yards in Yakima. All different tribes would go there from B.C. and Montana. There were Indians there living in tents. Every year many Indians go down, especially the Duncan and Nanaimo bunch. Mike Underwood always hired the hop pickers. He was well liked. We caught the CPR boat to Seattle and then caught the train to Yakima. I remember when we got to Yakima, we had to find our way to the hop yards. Some were lucky and caught rides. We managed to find a way as my brother Bill knew quite a few people, and we got a lift to the hop yard. We had to go to the boss to get a tent. There were no cabins in them days. My Aunt Molly went down with us with her granddaughter Connie Band that year. Her husband went up north fishing. My brother Bill took his son Wimpy. So I sometimes baby-sat these two, Wimpy and Connie. I enjoyed looking after them. After I finished working, they would follow me around. They were about seven years old. That was quite an experience for me, a young man, to work in a hop yard.

I found out a lot about hops. Malt, which is used in beer, is made from hops. They string wire six or eight feet up and tie the tops of the hops to the wire with string. When the hops grow they crawl almost to the top. They grow just like grapes. At harvest time, a vine is cut down and you have to pick it clean. So one guy goes along cutting the vines as you need them, others pick the hops off the vine and someone else cleans up the vines behind the pickers. The hops are put in sacks up to about forty pounds. It takes a lot of hops to fill a forty-pound sack. My brother Bill and I weren't very fast like some of those people, so we didn't make much money. The most we picked would be four sacks a day, about a hundred and sixty pounds, and we were getting two cents a pound. We would make a dollar sixty each a day working very hard. Big families could make money but with just Bill and I, we couldn't make anything.

We worked for a whole week. My brother Bill said, "Why don't we go and see the boss and get a day job?" So we went to see the boss. We told him, we want to stay here but we need a day job. Day jobs paid better, though the days were very long, usually from seven in the morning to six at night. They paid five or six dollars a day. There were different kinds of day jobs, such as driving the wagon to pick up the sacks, loading the sacks, weighing the sacks, or putting the hops in great big boxes for shipping to breweries. The boss looked at us and he said, "We need good strong men to put forty-pound sacks on the wagon." Bill got the job driving the wagon and I got the job throwing the sacks on the wagon.

We stayed there for about three weeks. It was a tent town. I'd say there were forty to fifty tents scattered all over. If you got there early, you got a good spot. We were late, so we ended up just at the bottom of a hill. We were given straw to put down for bedding. Some people had little oil stoves to cook on, others made their own fires. We had to bring our own groceries, just enough to eat as there was no place to store anything. We couldn't keep anything. There was always a lot of fruit in the Yakima Valley, such as watermelons and cantaloupes, which we could buy real cheap. Wagons would come around selling a whole sack of cantaloupes for seventy-five cents or watermelon for ten to fifteen cents each. The water wasn't good there so we needed this fruit.

At the end of the day, everyone would be very tired. We would go around and visit people we knew, but like the others we'd go to bed early. On Saturday and Sunday, we didn't have to work. This is when slahal games were played. It was a betting game. Every hop yard would have a game. Them Yakima Indians, Montana Indians, West Coast Indians, the Vancouver Island Indians had a lot of good players that knew how to play, and they bet a lot of money.

Brother Bill and I tried to promote slahal at our camp. I don't know how it happened but we got ourselves in a heck of a mess. We had to pay out. So that was the end of slahal for us. After that we just watched.

The women didn't play slahal, but they were the greatest blackjack players I have ever seen. They played for money and for blankets.

After I got back home, Dan Johnson, who is a relative of ours, asked me to go with him. I knew why he asked me, because we're good longshoremen, us Bakers. Joe Horton, the boss of the longshoremen, came to Westholme Reserve, near Duncan, and came to Dan's house. "Dan," he said, "do you want to go to work?" "No," said Dan, "I'm tired but I have a young man; he's a good longshoreman." So that was my first longshoring at fifteen years of age. I was big for my age. My first job was packing the stow lumber inside the ship's hatches. A sling load of lumber lying on a block is lowered into the ship. One plank of lumber at a time is put in a space carefully to get as much footage and tonnage in as possible. We had to make sure to butt each row. To "butt out" means when you put a plank down, like an eighteen-foot 2×4 or 2×6, the other plank might be eighteen foot, which makes thirty-six feet. So another fourteen feet would be needed if the hatch is fifty feet. If we didn't butt out properly, the lumber could shift around at sea and puncture the ship.

I worked three weeks there, getting a dollar thirty an hour. That was good money compared to what I was making in the hop yards. I had a couple of good cheques and headed for Nanaimo. I had an uncle up there I heard was looking for one man to go fishing with him. I went seining with him for a few weeks at Deep Bay, which is on Qualicum Beach. We didn't make any money. It was very slow. So in a short time I went from hop picking to longshoring to fishing.

The next year I stayed around home on the Capilano Reserve. I cut wood for a living — big fire logs. There used to be a couple of wood buyers. Sometimes we'd find a log drifting. Most of the time we went in the bushes here and we used to dig, dig down to some of the old logs. I guess they had logged that a few years before and they were buried, and we used to cut them stove length, and a cord was four feet wide, four feet high, eight feet long. We had three tiers of the eighteen-inch. Sometimes it would take us almost a week, maybe less, to cut one cord. We had to haul it quite a ways out, pile it on the road, then we had to go to the buyers. We used to get around four and a half to five dollars a cord. We had split it, and you stow it tight. The buyers always looked to see if there was any big holes or spaces, you know. That money we made, sometimes we had to split it three ways. Alfred was married then and he had his wife, but I was still single, and I used to get a dollar a cord. I made enough to live on, to buy a couple of ferry tickets and go to town, Vancouver. There was a guy that used to sell vegetables and fish in North Vancouver. And he used to sell ferry tickets, for a nickle each. Otherwise you had to pay ten cents, if you went and buy it at the wicket. So we'd buy two tickets for a dime and we'd go to see a show for fifteen cents, go play pool. And after a while I got away from them guys and used to go to the dance halls. I like to dance and I knew a couple of people. So I used to pay two bits to get in, and got acquainted with a lot of people, especially a lot of girls.

When I was seventeen I started fishing the Skeena. I went with my brother Bill. We had a twenty-four-foot two-man sailboat. My brother Bill ran the boat and I was the boat puller. I did whatever rowing had to be done. We had quite a routine. On Sunday evening at 5:00 P.M., we would throw our net in the boat and race out to the towboat. Towboats went up and down the Skeena right past the mouth of the river. You could get towed as far as you wanted. The towboat had a long line. We were always the first ones to get on the line, so we were in front.

When we would get to where we wanted to fish, we'd just pull our line, the boat steered off and we'd drift away and row to our fishing spot. We liked to set our net at 6:00 P.M. as we were just an hour away from the camp. We'd do this every day, except on Saturdays we'd quit fishing at 5:00 P.M. We would spend Saturday and Sunday mending our net, cleaning the boat and whatever else needed doing.

The towboats were really useful, because there can be twenty-four-foot tides in that part of the country. Mainly, the towboats were used to collect our fish. It didn't matter if you had two fish or a hundred fish, they would come by to collect them. They kept track of your catch in a tally book. At the end of the season they would count up everything, the amount of fish caught and what charges you had for groceries, clothing, boat and net rental. They used to give us books of tickets to use to buy things. You could get a ten-dollar book or a twenty-five-dollar book. After they figured everything out, in a good season, a boat puller could make a couple hundred dollars. My brother made more, because the one who runs the boat gets two-thirds and the puller gets one-third.

I liked working with my brother Bill even though he used to bawl me out if I did something wrong. Sometimes I slept in because I was tired. I had stayed out too long the night before. He really got mad at me when we got snagged. He used to blame me.

Bill and I worked in a sailboat, but they also have other types of fishing boats. They have the trollers (one-man boat), and they have the gill net (sometimes it's a two-man boat), but the seine boat, they have quite a big net on there, and they have six men to a crew with a captain, and they have a net that goes about three or four hundred fathoms. You make a round set that just goes down so many fathoms, and they have cable rings on the bottom that pull, pull the bottom in, and every fish in there is caught, so you pull all the net in until you get to the end, they call it the butt end, it was quite heavy. If you get a big catch you have to have a good net to hold that fish in there. You use a brailer to take the fish from the net and drop them into the hatch of the boat. Sometimes you get about anywhere from eighty to a hundred fish to one brailer. So if you had a big catch you get ten brailers, you know, you got a real good catch. But the seine is quite a thing, wherever you fish. Like at Deep Bay it is shallow; we had to cut our net down to half of what you use for the north and the deep water. So we always keep changing. The seine boat, you had bunks in there and you have a galley, and you always have one man that does the cooking. So you make about five, six dollars a day, and you try to work with the tide. You watch the fish where they jump. You get one jump, two jumps, you know you got quite a school of fish there. So that's a good life, that seining. It's five days a week.

I was glad when the weekend came because I had some free time then. My brother had his family there. The first year I usually went to the store with a bunch of young boys. We'd buy treats, then walk to a lake and do some trout fishing. We would also have races on the weekend to see who could put their net in the boat and get out on the towline first. My brother and I always won. He was really proud of me because I was strong.

The next year, I found other things to do. We would go to dances at the different canneries. The canneries were owned by different companies. There was Claxton, Carlisle, Haysport, Dominion, and others. I liked to go to dances where I knew some nice-looking girls. They had good bands and good musicians from Port Simpson, New Aiyansh, Greenville. Those Nass River people were all good musicians. Eli Gosnell, the father of the late James Gosnell, was a good musician, even if he only knew two songs, a waltz and a fox trot. Eli Gosnell played a saxophone. They had many different instruments, like pianos, banjos, guitars, saxophone and even trumpets. I liked to waltz, but I could two-step or do the chicken scratch. I never had trouble getting girls to dance with me. They knew I was a good dancer.

Well, I worked with brother Bill for a couple of years. The third year, I bought my own boat. I fished up there for about three years.

Then I came down to fish the Fraser River. That's when I got acquainted with the Wilsons. The Wilson family lived at Canoe Pass. Young Ivan, who was about my age, was a very smart-looking chap.

I remember one Armistice Day when we got the biggest haul of dog salmon. While we were pulling in the fish, I suddenly got very sick. It was an appendicitis attack though I didn't know it at the time. My partner had to cut the net and get to shore to get an ambulance to take me to the hospital. My partner knew I was in pain, and instead of waiting to get all the fish in, he cut the net. He hollered to someone to pack the fish while he called an ambulance. I got there just in time before my appendix burst. The doctor told me I was lucky to get there on time.

Another incident I remember in coming to Vancouver after fishing at Canoe Pass. I had made good money so I rented a room in the old Pennsylvania Hotel. I soon bumped into my brother Bobby and a couple of his friends. So I invited them up to my room. They had lots of beer with them. After a few beers, I left them and went dancing. There were two dance halls in Vancouver in them days. Lots of people, mostly single young people, went to these dance halls, which were really quite fancy ballrooms. They had good bands, big bands that would play fox trots, two-steps, waltzes and polkas. I danced with many different girls and often had more than one dance with those who were good dancers. A lot of the girls were there looking for boy friends and guys looking for girl friends. I never picked up any girls there. They were nice girls, but somehow I just went there to dance.

That particular night, after the dance, I walked back to the Pennsylvania Hotel. When I got to my room, a "Do Not Disturb" sign was on the door. I guess the guys drank all the beer up and fell asleep. Anyway, they wouldn't let me in, so I had to get another room.

The next day, a few guys and I went to Sumas. It was the end of the hop season and they were holding a sports weekend. My uncle was in charge of the sports. He asked me, "Nephew, do you want to box?" He knew that I was a pretty good boxer. These guys that I went with had a nice little roadster. We were just about out of gas and they were broke and I hardly had any money left. So these guys said, "Go ahead, Si, we need the money." I didn't know who I would challenge in the hop yard. I'd been drinking for a couple of days and I guess I felt I could trim anybody. Sure enough, I knew this guy they wanted me to box. His name was Lloyd. He was all dressed up in his nice boxing outfit. I took off my shirt, shoes, pants and just had my long johns on. It was in an open grounds. We went three rounds. My god, I didn't know how tough I was; there was blood all over, but I beat the guy. I got fifteen dollars for winning. I bought the gas so we could go home. I said, "It's the last time I invite you guys."

I finally came home in 1933. My grandmother said, "You better come home." So I did.

We Tie the Knot

I was back living in Capilano. One day in April, on my way home, I decided to take a short-cut across a little creek from the track right beside the graveyard and on past the home of Dennis Rivers. Dennis had a large family. One of his daughters, Emily, was eighteen years old. She worked as a housekeeper in Vancouver and only had Thursdays and Sundays off, from 2:00 P.M. to 11:00 P.M. On this particular day, Dennis Rivers invited me to stop in for a cup of tea. "Come on in, young fella, and have a cup of tea," he hollered as I was going by. I went in and visited for a while; then it was time for Emily to return to Vancouver. Dennis said, "Why don't you walk Emily to the ferry dock?" It was quite a way from the west end of the reserve to the ferry dock, so we had plenty of time to get acquainted. We had to pass a number of houses which faced the waterfront. I knew that people were looking out their windows and noticing that I was with a girl. There were quite a few single girls around and some of the mothers had their eyes on me. I guess they thought I was a good catch for their daughters.

My aunts Charlotte and Molly saw us walking together and I think they started the gossip that I was going to get married. That wasn't on my mind then as I was about to leave to go fishing up Skeena for two months. I saw Emily a few more times before I left to go fishing. I found her very friendly and

I could tell she liked me. She would tell me about her job. She really didn't like having so little time off. I told her about my experiences travelling around all over. We seemed to get along good. Somehow, I knew I was going to miss her. While I was away, I wrote to Emily a few times and she answered. I told her what I was doing, mostly about fishing.

My life changed a lot after I knew I had a girl friend at home. Before that I used to go out with every girl in every cannery. One thing I loved to do was get a bunch of kids together, the Wilson kids, who were nine, ten years old. I'd take them to the store, buy them candy. In them days, we didn't use cash out there. We were given vouchers. A book of ten tickets didn't last long when buying treats for a bunch of kids. I loved the kids and they really liked me. They kept me busy, too. But I still felt lonesome for Emily. I always told her in my letters, "I wish I was there with you." I was always happy to hear from her. She said she missed me and that she was always thinking about me.

In them days, I didn't have my own boat yet. I worked as a boat puller for the Wilsons and I got a one-third share. Once we finished fishing, we would have to mend the nets, fix up the boats and put everything in order. I was glad when we finished that season because it was just about two months since I'd seen Emily.

Emily looked surprised when she saw me, because when I left I was quite slim. During that two months, I guess I put on a lot of weight. I ate lots of fish and probably ate some sweet stuff with the kids. I was so huge that Emily could hardly get her arms around me. Anyway, she was happy that I was back home.

On Thursdays and Sundays, we'd see each other. We'd go for walks, sometimes to the Suspension Bridge. I liked those walks, holding hands, stealing a kiss behind a tree. We never did more than that because I had a lot of respect for her. I knew I was her first boy friend because her mother was very strict and never let her go around by herself. Her dad liked me so I guess that was why they let her go with me.

Once in a while, we'd go to a show or we'd visit her sister Thelma who lived on Dunbar. Having a few hours together, two days a week, wasn't much, and I knew she wanted to be with me more often. Me, I was busy with my own friends, with boxing, lacrosse and other sports, so time went by.

This went on all winter, and in the spring, when it was time for me to leave to go fishing again, we decided we couldn't leave each other for another two months. Emily asked me, "How about I go along with you?" Well, I had no money to pay for a wedding, and in those days people didn't just live together without getting married. Emily had been working steady since she finished school. She could only go to grade eight, the same as the rest of us. As a housekeeper, she made about twenty-five dollars a month. She didn't mind quitting her job as she was nineteen years old and didn't like being told she had to be in by eleven every night and could have a few hours off on Thursdays and Sundays. Besides, by then, we just thought we were made for each other. I was twenty-three, four years older than her, and it was time for me to settle down.

Her parents really liked me because they felt I wasn't like the other young guys around. I always liked to dress up, and I was a good athlete. They liked these things about me.

We decided to get married so she could go up the Skeena with me. She offered to buy the ring because she had some money saved up. We had a very small wedding at a United Church on Burrard Street in Vancouver. Tim Moody was our best man and Gertie Ettershank (Guerin) was the maid of honour. I had a suit to wear and Emily had a long peach-coloured dress that the lady she worked for gave her. She kept that dress for a long time.

After the wedding, we just drove around Stanley Park in Pete's car until about one o'clock in the morning. Pete was Emily's older brother. Emily had packed a little suitcase thinking we would stay in some hotel in Vancouver. Of course, I didn't have any money to speak of, so I couldn't go to a hotel. We didn't have any place to go. Gertie said we could go to her place and we could have her bed. Gertie and her family lived just two doors away from Emily's family. What a way — we started our lives on a borrowed bed near the bride's home.

Several days after we were married, they put on a little dance in our honour. The Squamish Band had an orchestra that played at dances every weekend during the winter at Catechism Hall on the Mission Reserve. Sometimes they went to play up Squamish or in the Fraser Valley. They were a real good orchestra. I can remember the ones playing at our wedding dance. There was Gus Band on the saxophone, Dominic Baker was the drummer, Stan Joseph played the banjo, Tim Moody on the clarinet and Andy Paull was the bandleader and he played the slide trombone. Chief Moses Joseph also played the saxophone and old man Dave Cole played the bass.

I always remember we had a good wedding dance. All the people on the reserve were there, our relatives and friends. As usual, the young girls from the reserve were there with their mothers. In them days, young women were not allowed to go to dances alone and young men couldn't take girls home after the dance. Parents, especially the mothers, were very strict.

Anyway, this was in June 1934, and people didn't have much money. We only got a teapot and a sugar bowl and a couple of other small presents.

After the dance, we had to walk home in the pitch dark down the tracks. Emily had high heels on. I had to make sure she didn't trip and fall.

The First Love Boat

Shortly after we were married, we left for Prince Rupert on a thirty-two-foot fishing boat, the *Seabird*, with Ed and Rose Sparrow from Musqueam. They had their five small children with them. I tell people this was the first Love Boat. We were honeymooners. Our honeymoon suite was on the deck between two forty-five gallon drums of gas and the stern of the boat. It was around the middle of June, a time when it was very hot during the day. It took us one day to reach Campbell River where we stopped for a few hours to visit my Aunt Emma at Cape Mudge. We also stopped for a short time at Namu where we went to the store to buy a few things.

It took us four days to go from Vancouver to Prince Rupert, travelling day and night. Ed and I used to take turns steering the boat. Emily would sit with me while I was steering. Otherwise, we would just sit on the bow of the boat and enjoy the beautiful scenery. At times, we'd play with the kids or catch some shuteye in our honeymoon suite. Ed and his family slept inside the bow and on the hatch between the cabin and the stern. The weather was just perfect. It was a beautiful voyage — a real honeymoon.

Emily's face was as red as a beet. She wasn't used to being out in the sun or on a boat but she never got seasick once.

When we got to Claxton Cannery near Prince Rupert, we were given a little cabin. These cabins were built for the fishermen and their wives. In our section there were about twenty cabins. There were others where most of the Nisga'a stayed and also cabins where the Japanese and Chinese people lived. Altogether there must have been seventy to eighty cabins at Claxton Cannery. There were about twelve canneries on the Skeena River. Claxton was the largest.

When we got to our cabin we were surprised to find two single beds. We were newlyweds. We didn't want single beds so we made them give us a double bed. We had pots and pans, dishes and all that we needed to take care of ourselves. Of course, being 1934, nothing was modern like today, but we managed all right.

Emily had a job at the cannery like most of the other fishermen's wives. They had machines to do some of the processing, but the women had to scrape the black stuff out of the inside of the fish. From about eight or nine in the morning, they would be on their feet until four or five in the afternoon, cleaning the fish. They had to work very hard because the fish were coming down the conveyor belt by the dozens. The women with more experience were given the job of cutting the fish, putting it in cans so that they could be sealed, then they were cooked.

One day during that summer we got a bad scare. There was a big fire in the middle of the week at the cold storage building. The cold storage was near the cabins and the cannery. Everything was close together. The cabins were in a row with nothing but bush behind. There was a road that went along by the cabins. At the end of the road there was a gas station. The fire was so bad that the people were asked to evacuate right away and not to take anything with them. Emily was among the group that had to run down the road toward the gas station. That was the only place they could go. It was a good thing the fire didn't spread from the cold storage. It burned to the ground.

The women and children were able to go back to their cabins. As they returned, they found bits of clothing along the road. I guess some people grabbed a few things from their cabins, then dropped them as they rushed along the road.

From where we were, all we could see was a large cloud of very black smoke. I got very worried about Emily. We rushed back to the cannery along with many other fish boats to find out what was happening. It was a relief to know that all the women and children were safe.

Usually, the fishermen were out from Sunday evening to Friday evening. I was always glad when Friday came and I could spend time with Emily. She would cook for us. We mostly ate fish and rice, but it was good. There would be dances on Saturday nights. It was a lot of fun. Emily liked to dance, too, so we would dance everything, the chicken scratch, polkas, waltzes, square dances, Charleston.

That summer was the biggest run of humpbacks. These are what are called pink salmon today. Anyway, one day I was busy throwing humpbacks from a big fishing boat for fourteen hours. There were about a hundred thousand humpbacks. When I got to the bottom of the boat, the humpbacks were as flat as my hand. There were too many for the canneries to handle. Seven or eight scowloads — barges — were sent to fertilizer plants. You would think with that much fish we could make a lot of money, but we didn't because we were getting only one and a half cents for each humpback. We got fifty cents a fish for sockeye. We only caught six hundred sockeye that summer — a very small catch.

It turned out that Emily made more money than me. We took a little fishing boat back home again to save the fifty dollars the cannery had given Emily for her fare to travel on the big boat.

We had a few dollars when we got home and bought a few things for the house and I got another job. I had to go to a camp over at Galiano Island, so we moved over there again for about a month and a half and I was getting seventy-five dollars a month. I had to work twelve to fifteen hours a day salting herrings and boxing them. Emily didn't work. The Japanese were so good to us, they used to come and give Emily a lot of things, different kinds of food that the Japanese made. Lots of rice. We used to get a big bowl of rice every day and that was something. We never refused to eat because we did like rice. Lots of salmons and lots of herring. We done well, so when we left there we went back home and that's when we settled down and we kept my grandmother there for a year. She was getting real old then, over a hundred years old. She was mostly bedridden and it was getting difficult for my wife to look after her and my brother Bobby who was also sick at that time. My Aunt Emma came there and knew the problem we were having, so she took my grandmother and took her down to my uncle Mathias Joe's place. And brother Bobby was put in the hospital because he was getting very ill; he had heart trouble, back trouble and was partially paralyzed, so that's why we had to put him in the hospital. And that's where he stayed until he died at the age of seventy-four. He was a very strong young man, but he got hurt working on the ship. He fell off the ship onto the dock and he hurt his spine and got paralyzed.

Raising a Family

In 1935, our first child was born. We named her Priscilla. She was one month overdue and weighed eleven pounds at birth. Poor Emily was only about a hundred pounds herself, so it was a very hard birth for her. She was in St. Paul's Hospital in Vancouver. She was in labour for over two days. I was really worried. I wondered why it was taking so long. In them days, the fathers couldn't go in with their wives. There wasn't even a place where I could wait in the hospital. So I had to walk back and forth from the CPR station. That was the only public place where I could sit and wait. Finally, at the last stages of her labour, Emily was given ether to put her out. Priscilla was born looking like a six-month-old baby. She had fat arms and lots of black hair. Emily had to get quite a few stitches and could hardly walk for the first two weeks. When she came home from the hospital, I had to help out with the housework. I remember doing the washing by hand. We didn't have an electric washing machine. I had to scrub on a washboard and wring things out by hand. I remember wringing out the baby blankets so hard that I tore them.

Priscilla had a lot of clothes because Emily sewed and knitted all kinds of things for her before she was born. We had everything for her, even a crib.

This was our first baby and she was roly-poly. I remember one day when Emily was dressing her on the table, she rolled off onto the floor. We were pretty scared, but it turned out that she didn't get hurt. I guess her fat protected her.

About a year and a half later, in 1936, Barbara came along. She was a normal-sized baby weighing seven pounds, six ounces. She was born at St. Paul's, too. It was August, and the canoe races were on and I was busy helping out. Someone came and told me that Emily had a girl, so I hurried over to the hospital to see Emily and the baby. Well, I stayed only about five minutes because I had to get back to the races. Later I found out that Emily was mad at me for not staying longer.

For quite a few years, I was really involved in sports, either lacrosse, boxing or canoe racing. Sports meant a lot to me, and if I wasn't playing, I was coaching or organizing tournaments — always doing something. I liked my kids and I was always good to them, providing a good home and food, but I was away a lot. I believe Emily felt like a sports widow many times.

In 1938, our first boy was born. We named him Kenneth Barry Simon. He was a nine-pounder. From the time we got married to after Kenny was born, we lived in the house I had built for my grandmother, brother Bobby and me in 1933. I always remember when I built that first house. In about 1931, my grandmother's nice house had burned to the ground. My brother Bill built her a three-bedroom shack which he put up in a hurry. I thought to myself, I'm a strong, young man, I should build a good house for my grandmother. In the back of my mind I also knew I'd want to get married someday, and what woman would want to move into a shack? But I didn't have any money to build a house. There was the big church that was built by my grandfather, Joe Capilano, and for some reason or another it never got used except by the Shakers people, before they built their own church. I thought it would be a good idea to tear it down and see what lumber could be used. I went to my uncle, Chief Mathias Joe, and asked him about it. He said, "If you want it, tear it down." It was April. The weather was good, so I went looking for a crowbar, a hammer and a ladder to get up on the roof. I started ripping the shakes, the shingles, off for firewood. I gave that to the elders. There was a lot of good lumber in the roof and walls of the building. Almost every piece of the siding came off easily because the nails were rusted.

The flooring was worn out. I piled it and let the old people take it away. Under the floor the timbers were very good. It took me almost two months to tear the old church down. By the time I was through, it was time for me to go fishing up the Skeena.

When I got back, I got my uncle and a few other men to help me haul the timbers and lumber. We used my uncle's two-wheel cart that he had built himself. It had wheels that were about three and a half feet in diameter with iron rims. Some men pulled the wagon and others pushed till we got all the lumber moved to where I was going to build the house. It was on the old Capilano Road near the PGE, the Pacific Great Eastern station. Today, the location would be on the corner of Capilano Road and Mathias Road on our reserve.

Most of the houses on the reserve were square with four walls and four rooms. I planned a different design, for a bigger house with an upstairs. I wanted an upstairs because the house was for my grandmother, my brother Bobby, who was not well, and Joe and me. Joe was away most of the time, but when he came back he always lived with us.

Bobby helped me by going to the mill at the foot of what is the Esplanade today to pick up all the shingles that were being thrown away. Any shingles that were under five inches to the weather, as they said, were thrown out. We hauled these shingles by canoe.

I gathered nails from wherever they were tearing down buildings and from the mill. From the salvage on Water Street in Vancouver, I bought windows and doors very cheap. The doors were a dollar fifty. I bet I spent no more than three hundred dollars on the whole house.

As our family grew, I worked on building a new house with three bedrooms on Marine Drive. The Squamish Band Council gave me a lot and a loan of three hundred dollars. I did all the work myself. Emily helped me quite a bit. I'd bring home lumber and she would help me make the window sills and other things. I was a longshoreman, so I could only work on the house in the evenings and on weekends. I even learned how to do plumbing so I could put in hot and cold water, bathroom and everything else. I was the first one on the reserve to have hot and cold water and a bathroom. It took me about a year and a half, but I got it finished and we moved into our comfortable new home in 1938.

Our family kept on growing. Pauline Eleanor, our third daughter, was born in 1939, weighing eight pounds, six ounces. In 1941, our second son was born, Peter Hugh Baker, eight pounds. The year Peter was born was quite a year. It was December 12, 1941, and just five days after Pearl Harbor was bombed. It was the time of the Second World War. It was also, sadly, the year my grandmother Mary Capilano died. She was around one hundred and two years old.

Our third son, Ronald Wallace, was born in 1942, nine pounds, twelve ounces. Nancy Irene, daughter number four, was born in 1943. She was eight pounds, nine ounces. All the babies were big, and Emily still stayed around a hundred pounds. Well, we figured this was our family. We had four daughters and three sons in eight years. Emily was very busy looking after the young children, the house, sewing clothes for all of us and looking after our small garden.

In 1941, Priscilla and Barbara started school together so that they could walk to school together. We didn't want to send them to no boarding school because I was working and we wanted them at home. We had quite a time to have them accepted into the public school. We finally got them admitted. Priscilla and Barbara were the first Indian children to be accepted into the public school. I had to struggle with Indian Affairs, the North Vancouver School Board, the West Vancouver School Board to get my children in school. Capilano Reserve, we were told, was in the West Vancouver School District, and where we were living on Marine Drive was in the North Vancouver School District, but still on the Capilano Reserve, which made it difficult to decide what school our children should go to. So they kicked them back and forth from West Vancouver to North Vancouver. They finally ended up at Capilano School, where we wanted them to go. I had to pay their tuition fee myself for two years to have my children go to the public school. I paid five dollars a month per child. I tried to get the Indian Affairs department to give me a refund but the agent said, "You set a good example and you should be glad to have your children in a public school." After that other Indians started to send their children to public schools in different parts of the province. In 1950, we were to have another daughter, Faye Rosemary Baker. She was a surprise, but an even greater surprise was when Charles Victor was born in 1959. By then a number of our children were married. That year, there were four women pregnant in the family: Emily, Kenny's wife, and our daughters Barbara and Pauline. Kenny's child, Sandy, was our first girl grandchild. Our first grandson was Priscilla's boy Billy.

All of our children went to public school and all the girls graduated from grade twelve. The boys were in a hurry to make money so they never finished school. They got jobs longshoring as soon as they could.

All our children got married. Some have been married more than once. Now Emily and I have thirty-four grandchildren and twenty-four great-grandchildren. I believe that we have done our part for the Canadian population.

Me at age nineteen

Emily Rivers at age eighteen

Playing tuba in the brass band circa 1928. I'm in the top row, far left. Among the others in the photo are Chief Joe Mathias, standing at far left, and Andy Paull, standing at far right.

Emily and me with our first child, Priscilla, in 1935

Easter Sunday, 1950, in front of our house on Marine Drive. *Left to right*: Me, Nancy, Pauline, Barbara, Emily and Faye

A Legend on the Waterfront

In 1935 I began my longshoring days, which lasted until I was sixty-five years old. I retired in 1976. Everybody knew me on the waterfront. At my sixty-fifth birthday party, people told my boys, "Your dad's got one of the biggest histories on the waterfront." They said, "He was one of the guys that everybody mentioned. He was like a hero or something." I believe I'm a legend on the waterfront for another reason. My grandfather Joe Capilano was the first Indian to be hired as a foreman. I worked my way right up to superintendent. Some of my boys have worked on the waterfront and now my grandson, Pauline's boy, has been a longshoreman for quite a few years. Five generations of our family have worked on the waterfront.

Our legend began in the late 1800s during the days of the sailing ships. They had one mill at the time on the North Shore. They hired all the Indians on the North Shore who were able to work. My grandfather became a foreman, which meant he had to look after men that were working there in gangs, including a lot of white men.

Sailing ships came from many parts of the world. They came from Hawaii, Chile, Argentina, West Indies, Portugal, Spain. You name it, they came here. Lots of sailors jumped ship in Vancouver and stayed. Many of them married Indian women from here. That's why in our reserves we have a lot of families named Gonzales, Corobello, Morales, Ratooms, Cordocedo. A lot of the families of these sailors also live in Victoria and Ganges on Salt Spring Island.

Long before I became a longshoreman, Indians from around here were working on the waterfront. I know that around 1926, there was a union called the Bow and Arrow. There were quite a few Natives in the union. In 1935, they went on strike. They lost, and the white people formed the ILA (International Longshoremen's Association). The shipping federation called a meeting of all the Indians. They told us, "If you guys want to get back, you guys better form your own gang — start working for the North Shore. Form your own union in North Vancouver. We'll give you your own gangs; we'll give you your own hall." So that's what we did. We formed the North Shore Longshoremen's Union. We were given six gangs and eighty sparemen, so there was plenty of work for our people. Later, the two unions amalgamated and became the ILWU (International Longshoreman's & Warehouseman's Union), 500.

Men who wanted to work as longshoremen just went to the hall at the waterfront. The foreman got to know which ones showed up regularly and they were the fellows that got picked first for the gangs each day. A gang was a group of eleven or thirteen men. If they were discharging cargo they had eleven men, but when they were loading they had thirteen men. When they formed a gang they had to have a hatch-tender — he was the leader. He was the one that looked after the hatch, rigging up the gear and supervising the men. He was the man on top that gave signals to pick up the load off the dock or scow and signals when they landed the cargo down the hold on the block. The yard arm and the mid-ship picked up the load, and the two winch drivers, they were the ones that drove.

They had a side-runner too. He was the one down below that made sure all the cargo was stowed right. They didn't want to blow — we always said "blow hole." Like in loading lumber, if you leave say five feet at the end, that's losing a lot of space. So the side-runner had to try and make the stowage fit tight. It was important to the ship. For safety. Always made it a tight stow, because in rough sea, when you roll, it could damage a lot of things. It was difficult for the hatch-tender to see, so they had to have another extra hatch-tender called a spareman to give signals to him. They used sparemen for lots of things. Sometimes they hired a couple of extra men to work with a gang.

I really worked my way up on the waterfront like anyone who wants to get ahead. Before becoming a foreman, I was a side-runner, a winch driver and a hatch-tender. When I became a foreman, I had an Indian gang, and I used to get all the big hatches.

I used to get all the good jobs on the ship, 'cause I had a good crew, they did good work. We could load lumber almost twice as fast as the white man's gang. That's the thing they used to say, the Indian gangs were good on logs, lumber, or anything like that. I was asked to be a foreman. Okay, so a lot of the guys and I drank every night. Sometimes someone got picked up for being drunk on the highway, but I quit that year I went bossing. I quit drinking. A lot of those white guys used to go to the head office, and they'd say, "Why did you hire that drunken Indian, what about us?" My boss said, "I'm not hiring a drunken Indian, I hired him 'cause he's a good longshoreman, good stevedore."

There were different stevedores in Vancouver: Empire, Canadian, Wolf and V & V (Victoria and Vancouver). I don't know how many stevedores they got now. Each stevedore had their own foremen and superintendents. When a ship came in, they picked their superintendent, who looked after the whole ship and four or five foremen. Each foreman was in charge of a gang. The superintendent worked with the supercargo. He was the one that got the list from the captain about what cargo got to board what ship, how many tonnage for each hatch. He told each foreman of each hatch how much tonnage they got and how long it was going to take them to load. The superintendent sat in the office and checked all hatches, tonnage, and knew how long it would take to unload or load because he knew whether the load was bulky or not. It would take less time to load a hundred and fifty tons of something bulky compared to thirty-six tons of smaller cargo.

So when you got to be a foreman or superintendent, they said you were going to boss. So I spent twelve years bossing both as a foreman and superintendent.

Earl Newman and I were the highest-earning workers of the Indians. Every year they used to check, the more hours you put in, the more benefits. A lot of our guys used to only work three days a week. This Earl Newman and I, the only time we missed work was when we had a funeral or were sick. Altogether, I spent forty-one years on the waterfront. The years I was bossing and my work with Vancouver Wharves did not count toward my pension in the ILWU 500. After I quit bossing, I found I needed three more years to make it twenty-five years in ILWU 500.

So I went to the union to see what I could do for my last three years. The guy comes to me and says, "Si, we're short of supercargo, how would you like to work at that?" I told him, "No, I have had enough worries as a foreman and I know what worries the supercargo has." I did work as a superintendent once in a while and I know I could have done the supercargo, but I was too tired to take it on at age sixty-two. They told me I could name any job I wanted. I took the job of tying up ships. It was a heavy job with long hours, pulling the big cables. After a month, I knew it was too hard on my body, so I went and told the boss I had to try something else. I became a checker, which was a very good job. I had to check every hatch, check the cargo, tell the drivers which bay to put their cargo in. All the cargo is numbered so we know what's going to Toronto, Winnipeg or Prince Rupert, wherever. I was a checker until I retired.

I learned a lot being a longshoreman. We handled all kinds of cargo like lumber, wheat, tallow, salmon, wool, alcohol.

Tallow was exported in barrels in those days. Now they ship it out in big tanks which you fill just like pouring wheat. Putting heavy barrels in the hold was much harder work. This animal fat was used for many things, like making soap. Sometimes a whole ship would be loaded with tallow.

Usually the alcohol came from Europe. They had Scotch, rye and other kinds of hard stuff. The wine and wool came from New Zealand and Australia. The Japanese shipped toys to different countries.

Of course, we shipped a lot of salmon — canned salmon, frozen salmon, salted salmon, to France, Germany, Spain, England and also Japan. Most countries wanted frozen salmon but the Japanese wanted mostly dried or salted salmon. The Japanese never really eat canned stuff.

There was a certain amount of pilferage going on. I used to do it like everyone else when I worked down below. Things like radios, fancy dishes and especially alcohol. Can you imagine! There were shiploads of whiskey. It was nothing for a guy to have two or three cases hid.

When I went bossing, I knew all the tricks. As foreman, I had to look after the cargo so I had to make sure nothing was being taken. One day I saw a guy go down in the hatch, I knew what he was doing. I didn't say anything. So when I went down, I checked. The guy had his lunch box full of three or four bottles of gin. So I went and filled all the empties with water, took all the full ones and put the ones with water in his lunch box. Oh my god, he had it at home for about a week. Then one night he had a bunch come to his house. He went to get his gin. They began to drink and someone said, "You trying to fool us?" He looked at me right away, he knew it must be me who did it.

I saw a lot of changes in the forty-one years I worked on the waterfront. When I first started we had to manhandle everything and we used to lift trunks or hand trunks down in the hold. At the time I became foreman, they began to use containers. The container ships were being filled right at the dock using big cranes. The big containers were lifted from ships, put on the dock and stacked by big fork lifts. Some containers were put right on railcars or trucks to take them to the Interior or down to the States.

Many jobs were lost when the containers started to be used. The union fought to discharge every container but it didn't work. Instead, the stevedoring shipping agents in Vancouver lost a lot of business to Seattle. Only local cargo kept coming to Vancouver. Seattle built up one of the biggest ports for containers.

After the union backed down, ships began to come to Vancouver again. I guess it's because it's closer and much easier to move the cargo out by railway or trucks from here. Quite a few men learned to be crane operators and how to drive fork lifts so they could keep working. Just like my boys Ronnie and Kenny. Ronnie is a good crane driver and he can run the fork lifts too. There's still a lot of work for men 'cause they got to have somebody there with the drivers, to assist the drivers. A lot of times there is still cargo that they have to manhandle.

Today, there's jobs on the waterfront for our boys, but a lot of young ones don't want to work. We could have a hundred men working there. The young men say they don't like the idea of going to the hall each day, sitting and waiting to be called to a gang. I tell them they have to work their way up. You just can't go up, well, my father was so-and-so, I want to get in the union. They got to put in so many years. Like my grandson, Pauline's son, now has been in there quite a few years, and finally going to get in the union. So when he gets in the union, he's set for life. He can go in the hall, pick his jobs, go to work whenever he feels like it; he'll work all the time.

They make good money as longshoremen, especially today. When I started I used to make about forty to forty-five dollars a week or, if I had a good week, fifty dollars. I always remember one time when I wanted to buy a car. So I had a good cheque; they used to pay us cash. I went over to Kingsway. That was the only one of the few places they sold cars. I saw this 1929 Model T Ford for forty dollars. So I bought the car, drove it home and I still had fifteen dollars left for groceries. After that I always had a car. I used to have a hell of a time with that Model T. I used to crank, jack the end up, let it run awhile, then shake the car and away I'd go. Everybody used to borrow it, too, to go to the hop yards. I'd charge them ten dollars. They would swear at it because they would get blisters cranking it up. That was the first car I got and later on I got another Ford. It was a 1936 model, a nice car, with automatic drive. I had trouble at first trying to use both feet, until I realized you should just use one foot. By the time I left longshoring, I was getting twelve to fifteen dollars an hour. That was a big change in forty-one years. In three hours, I could make what I made in a week in 1935. Now they get thirty to forty dollars an hour, more than double what I made.

Family and Business in the Forties, Fifties and Sixties

While in many ways the forties and fifties were great for me, this was the worst time for Emily in our married life. She was pregnant all the time, it seemed, and I was longshoring and involved with sports, mostly lacrosse. She would sometimes get a baby-sitter and come to watch a lacrosse game, but that didn't happen very often. I think, in a way, she hated lacrosse because I would be out two or three nights a week. Often, I'd get home very late. Emily would have my supper in the oven but it was usually cold by then. She was a good mother. She made sure the children were dressed well. She sewed most of their clothes. She always fed them on time even if I wasn't there.

I was drinking a lot too, then. I drank to be one of the boys, the longshoremen. When the fishermen came in, it was another celebration. We would all go drinking. At first it wasn't too bad. I'd go out one night a week with the boys; then it was two nights, and it just got worse.

Once in a while I'd take a week off work to go fishing. I'd tell Emily I wanted to make more money. Usually, I just wanted to get away by myself and have a bit of a holiday.

Those years were hard on Emily. I didn't realize it at the time. I remember getting home after one of those little fishing trips to find that all the kids had been sick. They had salmonella and had cried all night. Emily was really tired and gave me a bawling out for not being there to help her.

She also visited her mother every Sunday. She'd drag all the kids along with her. She really raised the kids herself. She made them new outfits for Easter. She spent all summer sewing clothes for them for school. I remember that her first sewing machine was secondhand. Later she was able to buy a new one.

One thing we did as a family and still do to this day is celebrate the birthdays. We were never short of food, so we had a special meal and birthday cake and gifts for the birthday gatherings. We had a small garden that we were both to look after but I must admit she did most of the work. It was good to have some fresh vegetables.

In 1958 I put on a giant powwow with dancers from other provinces. It was a great event. It was so good that I had plans to have an even bigger and better powwow the next year. It didn't happen because of a serious health problem. I had a sudden setback in 1959 when Emily was pregnant with Charlie. I got very sick at work one day and I had to be taken to the hospital. Very suddenly, my left testicle had swollen to the size of a baseball. The doctor diagnosed me with prostate cancer. When they told me, it was like someone shot me. They said they would have to operate immediately. Emily was so shocked by the news that she went into labour and Charlie was born. We were both in Lions Gate Hospital. She was on the top floor and I was on the bottom floor.

Well, I guess you could say my operation was a success. But they told me I had to receive cobalt treatments. They found a lump on my chest as well and treated it with cobalt. It would make me very sick. I had a hard time eating because everything seemed to taste like rust. I couldn't go longshoring for the better part of a year. Emily took a job at Ranch Restaurant, cleaning chickens for three or four hours in the evening. It helped to pay our bills. I went back to work, but it was ten years before I was totally cleared up from the cancer and cobalt.

In 1960, we had to move from our house on Marine Drive. We had been in that house from 1938. We had put a lot into it and

Emily had a nice garden. The Band told us that we would have to move because there were plans to widen Marine Drive. We didn't like the idea but we had to do it. The Band was compensated for the house, and the money was used to build the house we are in now. Our house we moved from was where the International Plaza building is now.

I had lots of time to think during the year I was sick. One idea I had was to start a family business. It took quite a while to get everything together, but in 1965, I opened the Big Chief Drive-In in Brackendale. It was in a beautiful location near the water and just a few miles from Vancouver on the newly built Squamish Highway. I had the idea that people would drive up during the weekend and stop at our drive-in.

Every Saturday morning, we'd pack our stock of potatoes, hamburger meat, onions, pop and chocolate bars into our car and head to Brackendale, which is about sixty miles from Vancouver. Nancy, Faye and Charlie, our three youngest, would be along. The girls helped us a lot by peeling potatoes for our french fries. All I can remember about Charlie, who was only six when we got started, was that he ate a lot of the french fries.

We'd open up by about ten in the morning. Quite a few people would stop for a snack. The main attraction was the Indian show I'd put on in the afternoons. I'd put on my big headdress, buckskin jacket, moccasins, bells and do a number of dances. I'd explain my talking stick and get people involved doing the deer dance. Oh, they really enjoyed it. I believe quite a few people came up from Vancouver with their children just to see the show. I never charged for the shows, but I'd put a basket out with a sign saying "Give to the poor Indians." Some people did leave money. I had told the kids that whatever money was in the basket would be theirs and at the end of the summer they could buy something. Well, after each show, they'd run to look in the basket. Sometimes they would be very disappointed because there would be only a few cents in it. I decided to put the basket on a pole so they couldn't see in. In the end there was enough for each of them to get a bike.

Big Chief Drive-In lasted for three summers. We tried to make a go of it, but it was hard. It meant that I worked all the time. I was longshoring, so when we'd close at about seven on Sunday evenings, clean up the deep-fryer and everything, it was pretty late. Then we'd drive back to town and I had to be at work early Monday.

Emily had a lot to do, too, because she ran the drive-in, cooked the food and before that had to shop for our weekend supply. So we decided after three summers to lease it out. Well, I always say, it's hard for others to run your business. It didn't work out. In the end my good idea cost me a lot of money. I guess you could say I lost my shirt in the deal. I had borrowed seven thousand dollars from the Band to build the drive-in and I put in the rest of the money. In 1975 I got the job of Band Manager. During the time I worked there, I had the Band take money from my salary and I paid back the whole seven thousand. I'm proud that I did that because I don't believe in not paying your bills. I can say that I don't owe anyone a cent right now.

I was involved in putting on powwows for many years. It was a way to share our culture with non-Indians. In those days not much was going on. It seemed our people were forgetting their ways and just living like white people. That's why I used to put on powwows and bring Indian dancers and singers from different parts of B.C. and sometimes I invited Indians from other provinces. I spent a lot of my time organizing and running these powwows.

When the children got older, Emily would set up a little stand at the powwows and sell souvenirs like small totem poles that Chief Seagull sold to us for a good price. She made some money on this and started to collect a small stack of crafts in our basement. People knew we had crafts for sale. Our son Peter suggested to his mother that she open a store to sell crafts. Some of the other sisters and brothers thought it was a good idea and said they would help. It would be a family store. Peter got his friends together and they began to build a little store right next to the house. He got a loan of three hundred dollars from the bank for his mother.

In 1971, the family opened the store. It looked like a little shed. We called it the Bakers' Store. Marlene, Ronnie's first wife, did the buying, but she didn't last very long. She came in one day to help and sold only one card and that was it. So one by one the family drifted away. Emily decided that since she was pretty well working alone in the store, she would change the name from Bakers' Store to Khot-La-Cha. I was glad when she took my Indian name for the store. Khot-La-Cha is my Squamish name given to me by my grandmother. It means "Man with a Kind Heart." She said I would be a man who would look after his people.

The store was one of the ways we could serve our people. Emily bought carvings of cedar and silver jewellery, leather crafts, Cowichan sweaters and socks, beaded earrings and many other crafts from different Indians. All kinds of people would visit the store. Some were our own people; sometimes a whole busload of tourists would stop by. It turned out to be a good business, but it was another thing to keep Emily so busy that she wasn't free to go around with me. It seems she is such a good worker that she always had to be very busy. First it was the children and the house, then it was the store. She struggled alone with that store while I was travelling here and there in Canada and other countries.

Emily had to hire different people to help her in the store. Most were family members. In 1988, Emily had health problems and it was getting harder and harder for her to run the store. We talked about it and thought she should sell it. Well, of course, the store is right here on our property and that would kind of make it hard if an outsider owned it. Anyway, we thought that an Indian should buy it, either someone from the reserve or someone in the family.

One day Nancy, our daughter, asked her mother all about the store. She was considering buying it. At the time, Nancy had a good job with B.C. Tel. She said she'd quit her job and just buy the store business. I know Emily was very happy that Nancy was interested in taking over. So Nancy bought the store and Emily is now a part-time employee, which suits her. The store was her life for many years and it would have been hard for her to give it up altogether. This way, she doesn't have the responsibility of managing it and yet she can help. She is free now to come and go as she pleases.

I do a lot to promote the store. When I'm asked to go to open meetings, conferences, I tell them about Khot-La Cha Arts and Crafts.

Somehow, we managed to raise our family and stay together for sixty years. Our sixtieth anniversary was on June 7, 1994. I always say that I had a good wife who took care of our home. She was tough on me, too, I guess that's why I pulled through some of my crazier times, like when I was drinking a lot. She would say she was going to leave me as soon as the kids got big. I stopped drinking just before our youngest son Charlie was born in 1959. I guess I knew he would be our last and if I kept up a wild life she might take off.

As I said earlier, my drinking over quite a few years was getting worse all the time. One night I got picked up by the police when I was on my way home. I guess I was pretty loaded. That night Emily had called her sister late at night to ask her if she had seen me in any pubs. She told Emily that she should call the police. Well, I guess she still waited, and about an hour later I called her from a jail in New Westminster. I had no money and no car. She had no way of getting to New Westminster to bail me out. I finally called my boss and he came and bailed me out. I felt really bad that time. It was the first time I ever landed in jail and thank goodness it was the last, because I decided it was time I joined A.A. It wasn't easy at first to change my lifestyle, going out to drink with the boys after work. Emily helped me a lot. She would always come with me to the A.A. meetings at first. We were finally doing something together.

I managed to be busy even after work, always doing things for everybody else. Somehow, I seemed to like that. I guess I still do that these days, though I am at home a lot more. It's in my blood and it is what I believe I'll be remembered for. Most of what I did was good, like the powwows, the trips, the committees and clubs I served on. I just didn't take the same kind of time for my family.

Now the kids are all fathers, mothers and even grandparents themselves. We all get along good. I thank the Great Spirit many times, now that I am an elder, for keeping us throughout our lives.

The Last of the Famous North Shore Indians

I like most sports, but lacrosse is our game. Lacrosse is a real Indian game. They played lacrosse a lot back east. It started in Quebec, then moved on to Ontario and British Columbia. They played field lacrosse until 1932. There were good athletes. They used to play it one tribe against the other tribe and the last one that was left on the field or walked away from the field, they were the winners. They used to club each other, do everything. They just went ahead, and whoever was able to stand up at the finish, that was how they won. That was how come some of the greatest lacrosse players in Canada were Indians. They were from Six Nations, St. Regis and the North Shore. They're all gone. I'm the last, they say, of the famous North Shore Indians. I'm the last of that bunch.

Box lacrosse started in 1932. That was the year that we were all playing baseball and we gave up baseball to go and play box lacrosse. The first game we played was at the old horse show building at the Pacific National Exhibition when the floor was dirt. The building is still there, just west of the racetrack, where they have horse shows. We didn't play there very long because of the dirt floor. We might as well have played outdoors. This was before the arena, the Hastings Forum at the PNE, was built. The arena had a board floor. We used to enjoy playing quite a bit. In 1932, it was mostly all the Bakers playing. There was Henry "Hawkeye" Baker, Ray, Dominic, Frank, my brother Bill and myself. Bobby didn't play. He played field lacrosse before he got hurt. Also, there was Louie Lewis, Gus Band, Stan Joseph, Chief Moses Joseph, Freddie and Joe Johnson, Ducky Mack and a few others. That was the family. We were all related. When we won the championship we had four non-Indians playing with us. We went as far as Winnipeg. We won at Calgary but we lost out at Winnipeg. We couldn't get nobody to sponsor us, but one of the guys from New Westminster, the commissioner, managed to raise enough money for us to make that trip to Winnipeg. In 1932, that was the year of the Depression. Nobody was working, and I was lucky if I had thirty-five cents when I left Vancouver. A lot of us hardly had any money but we always managed to get a few dollars. But we did win a championship, because we all played the game together. We had nothing else to do but play lacrosse behind the church. We used to practise and practise and that's how we became famous in lacrosse. We used to pass that ball, push it in circles real fast. We were good stick handlers. That's how come we used to beat them guys, and the best part of it was that we all talked Indian and when we hollered in our language the white man would look, and when he looked the other way, we were gone. They used to really swear at us Indians talking our own language. Nineteen thirty-two was the first year we won the B.C. championship, but then we broke up because we couldn't get enough money from a sponsor.

In the old days when we played there were four teams there for a while and then another team came in, so we had five teams that played in the intercity league. There were the Salmonbellies and Adanacs from New Westminster; Burrards, who were first called the Bluebirds, from Vancouver; the Richmond Farmers, from Richmond; and the North Shore Indians. The North Shore Indians were the biggest drawing card of all the teams. Every time that the Indians played they had a full house. This was the case even when we started to lose. When I first started I was, oh, about twenty-one years old. Already most of our players were ten or twelve years older than I was, so you can imagine how they kept it up. In the last year I played, before I got injured, I was in my best condition both physically and mentally. I used to train very hard. I never smoked or never drank all through the lacrosse season. That was one thing that I respected, not only the team but my body.

I was still playing when I got married. I was away from home quite a bit. Emily used to come with me once in a while, but she didn't like lacrosse because I used to be out for maybe two or three nights a week going to New Westminster and Richmond. We had quite a schedule every year, and we really worked hard. What made it very difficult for us, the North Shore Indians, was that every one of us was playing at the time we were longshoremen. We used to work ten-hour days. Imagine, in those days we used to work down the hole carrying lumber. It was heavy lumber, and after those ten-hour days we used to go play lacrosse the same night. We used to wonder how we ever did it, but I kept myself in good condition. Some of the others were starting to fade away. They were getting old and their bodies couldn't take it much longer, but they still did a lot of handling with the lacrosse stick and knew how to play their positions. It was because of that teamwork that we used to win. We would pass that ball from one player right clean around and then when we'd get a man in position he would be the one that did the shooting and scoring. So we were very well trained. We used to holler, talk Indian, and know our position. We knew what we wanted. I used to play forward but after a while, when the old guys couldn't get back to play defence, that's when I played defence, and I really worked hard. I always remember, Henry, Dominic and I used to watch the older guys, and in the third period they just didn't have enough strength to go out there and give it all they had. Sometimes I had to look after two men before the other guy would get down, and my cousin Hawkeye, the goalie, was waiting for him. Henry won best goalie award. Chief Moses was "the fastest man on two feet," a good sprinter, and I won rookie of the year.

In 1933 and 1934 there were five or six of us playing for the Salmonbellies. In 1935, Andy Paull, the manager, got busy and he got some money and got all those boys from the Six Nations. There were the Bomberrys, the Smiths, the Squires, and we still had most of our boys that were able, so we got our franchise back, and once again the North Shore Indians were a good team. Nineteen thirty-six was a great year for the North Shore Indians. We won the B.C. championship and I played hard, but at the time of the playoffs I got in a car accident. I injured my back so I couldn't go back to the team or do anything. They drew the biggest crowd at Maple Leaf Gardens in Toronto. They had all the Six Nations there. They almost filled the Maple Leaf Gardens. It was two out of three games and after one game they took our boys to a party one night at Six Nations, and I think that's how come they lost. But Conn Smythe, the owner of the Toronto Maple Leafs hockey club, commented that he took note of the combination passing used and wanted to integrate it into hockey.

We tried again after that. Andy Paull was a great promoter. He promoted a professional team and took a bunch of players down to Los Angeles. Joe E. Brown, the famous comedian, sponsored the team. It was there that they met Tonto. He was Harry Smith at the time and was one of the greatest lacrosse players, and then he became an actor all of a sudden and took the name Jay Silverheels. Well, they played a good game down there, and when they came back to Vancouver they were barred from playing amateur lacrosse because they played professional down there. After that we couldn't use many of our boys to play amateur, so the team became half Indian and half white.

I worked with Andy Paull quite a bit in my young days. We did a lot of canvassing. I used to watch Andy. How that guy used to work. My god, he could manoeuvre people around. He knew how to talk to people, how to convince people. You know, I think we won two games that he protested. We won those games in the committee room. That's how good Andy Paull was. He was like a lawyer. He was why a lot of people had respect for the North Shore Indians.

In 1939, we had to give up our Senior A franchise. We were told, "When you Indians are ready, you can have your franchise back." So because our players were older and those who played professional one year couldn't play Senior A, my brother Dan and his sons started the Senior B team. I was president of the league we formed with Six Nations in 1970. Les Johnson was the general manager. We'd have games one year in the west and the next year it would be in the east.

The Senior B League grew to quite a few teams. Russ Powless later became league president. He was from the east. He had it for quite a few years. Brother Dan became president after he got sole ownership of the Capilano Trailer Court and could afford to sponsor the league. After he died his son Frankie Baker took over ownership and presidency. He owns the North Shore Indian Lacrosse team today.

In 1993, the North Shore Indians Senior B won the President's Cup. After that they decided to apply to the Western Lacrosse Association to get their Senior A franchise back. So after many years we are back with the original group, except there are no Richmond Farmers. But there are still five teams in the Senior A League. We trained a lot of fellows in the Senior B and I believe they're ready for Senior A.

In 1967, they got a Hall of Fame for lacrosse players. It's in New Westminster. The teams in the league worked hard on this. A committee was put together to see who would get into the Hall of Fame. They checked the records. That's how Henry Baker, called Hawkeye, got in the Hall of Fame. He was the greatest goalkeeper. He played goalie in an all-star game in Los Angeles.

Ray Baker also got in the Hall of Fame. He was the high scorer in the league. They called him "the old fox." The latest North Shore Indian to get in the Hall of Fame was Stan Joseph, Jr. He was a goalkeeper, too, later than Henry "Hawkeye" Baker. They picked the players who were always in the sports headlines. I was proud of my cousins.

When Ray was inducted, he asked me to go and speak for him. Stan Joseph also asked me to go to his induction. I spoke for him, too. The team that has most of the players in the Hall of Fame is the Burrards, because they had always been the outstanding team every year. The Salmonbellies, Richmond Farmers and Adanacs had a couple of good years as well. I remember the Adanacs when we first started playing. We used to beat them 32 to 6. A couple of years later they just turned around and scored the same thing against us. At that time they were all young, good-conditioned players and most of our boys were getting old. We couldn't last forever.

I believe Andy Paull should have made it to the Hall of Fame. He was an outstanding coach.

The Mann Cup is the treasured trophy of the Canadian Lacrosse Association and represents Senior lacrosse supremacy. I think our boys will have a good chance of bringing it to the North Shore this year.

Every year I go to lacrosse games, mostly the Senior B because that's where our boys are playing. I always feel we should train our younger ones and get back in the top league, the Senior A. If we can get good players who can score goals, we could have lots of action and get some excitement going like in the old days. We need our Squamish boys in there. There's more interest because of winning the President's Cup in Senior B. I think our young fellows will do a good job in 1994 back in Senior A.

I know I'll be there encouraging them. They have to look after their bodies to be strong. That's what I tell them.

This is something I believe I practised when I first got into sports. I knew I had to condition myself, my body, my mind. When I was ready, felt ready to compete, my mind was in good shape, my body was in good shape, everything. We all respected each other. No one was just an individual. We played as a team. We played as a team to win. My belief to respect and to train was due to my early upbringing. My grandmother said to put my body in condition — to walk, to run, to train. I was trained physically and mentally. It was something I really learned and worked at. I was not an outstanding athlete, but I was an athlete in that I could hold my own and really challenge anybody. In that way I have always been outstanding. I was never a goal scorer but I was a good regular player, because I worked as part of a team. In a spiritual way, I know there is somebody there coaching. I knew I had to run a mile, skip, exercise, and I had to watch what I ate. I had to quit drinking when I was training. I was a good athlete. I played the game; I played it clean and my mind was satisfied, win or lose.

Before we got into lacrosse in 1932, this same bunch that were on the lacrosse team, all the Bakers and my cousins, were involved in other sports. We had a pretty good baseball team. Our league had five teams: Native Sons, Merchants, Lynn Valley, North Shore and West Van. We used to play at Mahon Park. We had good players and we won a lot of cups. I always remember Bill Gallagher from Powell River, who was a great pitcher, very fast. I was a catcher during practice so I knew how hard he could throw. My hand would be red from catching the ball.

Andy Paull was the one who got us involved in all different sports. Besides baseball, we were canoe pulling. We used to race canoes and competed in a lot of festivals for about two years. We won one year in Victoria.

I also played one year for the North Shore Cougars football team. We won the B.C. Junior League that year. I didn't keep playing because that was when I was fishing. They were sorry to see me go.

Another sport I really liked was boxing. I used to watch all those great boxers like Joe Louis, Tod Morgan. A lot of good fighters came from Vancouver, lightweights and all. I boxed quite a bit myself. I used to go and watch them boxing, to learn.

I used to paddle across in my canoe and go to Harrison's. Catch the streetcar to Hastings East to the Italian Centre. Sometimes I'd go all the way to Richmond. I boxed heavyweight. I remember busting a guy's ribs. We used to have a club at Davie. We had an amateur club up here in Capilano. We'd help raise funds for a building. I boxed for about two years. I did a lot up Skeena. There were good fighters up there from Hazelton, Port Simpson. We had competitions between the Fraser River and the North.

My grandmother would look at me when I'd come home, with a broken nose, black eyes. She'd say, "Why do you do it? Why do you want to fight?"

I still like sports. I go to as many games as I can, whether it's lacrosse, football or hockey. I go to canoe racing festivals. I watch sports on TV. I always think, if I had been a sports star, professional, I would have liked it to be in lacrosse because that's our game.

An early lacrosse team made up of my brothers and cousins. *Back row, left to right*: Henry "Hawkeye" Baker, Moses Joseph, Louie Lewis, Frank Baker, my brother Bobby Baker. *Front row, left to right*: Gus Band, my brother Bill Baker, Ray Baker

Here I am in 1936 in my North Shore Indians jersey, with a friend.

Henry "Hawkeye" Baker, 1936

The North Shore Indians Old-Timers team, 1940. *Left to right*: Joe Jerome, Chief Moses Joseph, Tommy Cole, Vic Guerin, Earl Newman, Dominic Baker, Cliff Paull, Stan (Si) Joseph, Hawkeye Baker, Ted Band, Fred Johnston, Stan Bomberry, Joe Johnston, Harry Newman, Hub Smith and the great Andy Paull. Kneeling in front are Bill Baker and Ray Baker.

On the waterfront with a fellow longshoreman, 1957

Working with My Band

I look at the Squamish Band today and see the houses, many of them even better than those owned by white people in North Vancouver. Everybody on our reserves has running water, indoor toilets, electricity. Everybody pretty well has microwave ovens, VCRS, you name it. Lots of people have modern cars, some have more than one car.

This is good. I always wanted my people to have everything like the white man. We had to fight hard for those things. Young people today don't realize how us old-timers worked in them days, about fifty years ago, to get what we have today.

In my young days, we didn't have those things. We lived in shacks with outside toilets. We used coal oil lamps and wood stoves. Most of our clothes were homemade from old clothes given to us by white people. We didn't seem to know that we could have things, the same as the white man.

It wasn't until I was a young man and travelled to other places in B.C. that I realized we could do better, that we could have running water and electricity. Indians didn't have to live like we were. I had to leave the reserve to find out how people live. All reserves seemed to be in the same condition. I found out we had to improve our homes, go out and look for the material, do a good day's job and earn your pay and put aside so much of your pay to improve your conditions.

Our Band didn't have much say about how we wanted things on our reserve. It was all run by an Indian agent who controlled everything. It was like we were little kids and couldn't think for ourselves. But we didn't know any better; we just did what we were told.

We had hereditary chiefs in the early days, even in 1940s when I started to get involved with Band meetings. The traditional hereditary chiefs system changed when some of the chiefs had no sons to take over from them. They made a rule that when that happened someone would be elected as a lifetime councillor. I got elected in 1942 and I'm still a councillor till I die, even though I don't go to many meetings any more.

Mostly our Band meetings would be in the evenings or on weekends. Some Squamish people lived up Squamish, so they came when important decisions had to be made. It was better then to meet on Saturday or Sunday when people were not working.

In them days, the meetings were chaired by the Indian agent and we always more or less had the same agenda. We talked about welfare, housing. Later, we got into development. I tried to get issues on the table to educate the council. I knew we had to do something about employment, to get work for our people. The Indian agent always tried to control things. He wasn't only the chairman of our meetings but he was also the treasurer, and we never seemed to get any reports from him.

I thought there must be some way I could contribute, to ask the people of my Band, "Can we do this? We have lots of land, the people are using our land and we're getting just a little rent money." That's the money I was trying to get the Indian agent to give us, the money so we can live like white people. Any time you read about Indians in the newspaper, it tells about the poor conditions our people are living in. That was what was always in my mind.

I worked for a lot of people outside the reserve. They would encourage me. They'd say, "Simon, why don't you people do something?" We had the land. I tried to buy books and I even tried to go back to night school to learn about economics, but I couldn't manage to work every day and go to school too.

The Indian agent always said that what I was asking for would take money. I knew we had money from the sale of land and gravel. Fifty per cent went to distribution, twenty-five dollars per person, which was given to us at Christmas time; the other 50 per cent went into our capital account.

I asked Mr. Ball, the Indian agent, how much money we had in our capital fund, when we could get it and what we could use it for. He said, "Well, I don't know, but whatever you take out will affect your distribution." So I said to him, "I get twenty-five dollars, my wife gets twenty-five dollars, and the next day we're broke and many of our people still don't have no running water, no lights."

Finally, he told us that we had $800,000, but if we took it out we'd lose our distribution. I told him it would help our people much more if we all had sewers, water and electricity.

Our council was glad to know we had money. So we formed a committee to plan how we should use the money. We decided to ask for half of our money, $400,000. Just at that time, they were getting rid of wartime houses. Somebody came and told me, "Gee, Si, we could buy these wartime houses. They come in three sizes, singles, doubles and those with an upstairs, for two hundred, three hundred and four hundred dollars." We figured out how many houses we could get from our money, including the sewer and water. So we got so many houses. They wanted us to have a boulevard. To build a boulevard would have cost us $500,000. This guy who was advising us was from the university. I said to the council, "Let's get rid of this guy. We don't need him. Let's do it ourselves." So we did. We had meetings late into the night many times.

Things changed a lot for us when Mr. Anfield became our Indian agent. He was the senior teacher at Lytton when I was going there. He remembered what I used to do as a leader at the residential school. I figured he would be a good agent because he respected us even as students.

Not long after he became our agent, he told the council, "I want you to know that this is the last meeting I am going to be chairman. You have to pick out one of your councillors to be chairman. I would like to just come over here and make my presentation and let you people handle your own business. You decide what you want to happen." We were surprised to hear him say that, because Indian agents before him seemed to want to control everything and have us councillors rubber-stamp what ideas they had.

So when the council heard Mr. Anfield, right away Chief Moses spoke up and said, "I nominate that young man over there, Simon Baker." Well, someone seconded it right away and no one else was nominated. So I became the chairman in 1965 and was chairman for ten years before I retired. All the time I was the chairman, which was the chief councillor, I worked with committees. I formed committees in economic development, education, welfare. Most of the old councillors, they all listened, they like to learn. Many of them never been anywhere, never left the reserve, never knew what was outside. Me, I'd been travelling and was off the reserve for quite a few years before I came back. I had a good idea about things. I associated with people during that time that either graduated or became lawyers, doctors, developers, you name it. That's when they started coming to me and asking me what we were going to do with our land. The Capilano and Mission reserves are surrounded by the city, municipality and districts, and that was the only land available for development. We had so many people apply to lease or rent some of our land. So I brought it to the council one day. I said, "You know, we have millions of dollars in resources on our reserve and we have to do something about it and I want to know what you guys think. Do you think we should start doing something?" They laughed when I said millions of dollars. "I think what we should do is get a legal advisor," I told them. Everyone started talking then. One of the councillors said, "I think we should form a committee. We'll look around for a legal advisor."

That was when we hired a young man who had already been working in Ottawa for a few years since he graduated from economics. So he had a good idea of what we were talking about when we talked about land, but he didn't have much knowledge of the land claims. This is what we taught him. We said we had to go to Ottawa. He knew who we should approach; he knew the people there and he knew who would be able to help us. By god, things really started moving! We had an economic development committee that I chaired. I was chairman of Kapilano 100, Park Royal Committee. We were working on the leasing of our land to Park Royal. I can say, today, I lived long enough to see the revenue for our people from some of those big leases.

I wanted women to be leaders because they had a lot to say at meetings. I appointed some women to chair the committees. We got things moving pretty well but we didn't have people with much education or training, so it was hard for them. Many had never been away from the reserve. I tried to encourage them to further their education, get training, but I guess we were just too busy trying to run our Band business.

During those years, we had a lot of things to work on. We were trying to get compensation for cutoff lands. About a hundred and thirty acres of land worth over two million dollars had been cut off by a commission for private enterprises. We had a housing plan to build 127 units by 1975. We were working on quite a few leases with Twin Theatres, Park Royal Towers, Park Royal Shopping Centre, International Plaza. We had education, welfare, and our whole administration to look after.

Times are changing now and it is getting better. We have people who know business, and when we have to, we hire people who have the training from outside. But they work for us. No more Indian-agent style.

It was hard being chairman for our council. There was so much to learn and so much to do. Overnight, there were many people working for the Band. As time went by, it seemed that things got out of hand. So I asked the council to appoint people to be an executive committee to help me. They named three people, one from Capilano, one from up Squamish and one from Mission Reserve.

We tried to make sure everything would go right. It was a difficult time for everyone. We couldn't seem to get anywhere with anything we tried. I had the idea all the time that we could run our own office and business, but somehow there were many problems to deal with.

At that time, I was still working on the waterfront for Vancouver Wharves and trying to be chairman at the same time. It meant I had two full-time jobs and a family to look after. No wonder I never did much with my kids, though by then they were pretty well grown up. I hardly remember their teenage years.

I guess I nearly had a nervous breakdown. I felt the pressure in trying to carry on the work as chairman of our council. I had another problem with Vancouver Wharves. They wanted me to move from Canadian Stevedoring, which I did. What I didn't know was the reason they wanted me was because they wanted a piece of property owned by our Band. They thought that by getting me to work for them I could get the Band to give up the property. I had no idea of us giving up that piece of land, but I felt the pressure. I also didn't like working with the sulfur. I used to be up to my knees in it. This was dirty work, but they wouldn't give me a better job that I wanted. It was a hard time in both of my jobs, so I began to pull out from everything. The boss at Vancouver Wharves seemed to know something was wrong with me. He said, "Chief, I know you are sick or something is bothering you. I'm going to send you to my doctor for a complete checkup." I went for the checkup, and after the results came in the doctor said he didn't find anything wrong with me, but he said, "What you must do is get away from your work at the waterfront and with the council. You have to tell your wife that you must go away by yourself for a complete rest." I told Emily what the doctor said. She said right away, "Why don't you go and visit Nancy?" Nancy, our daughter, was married and living in Corpus Christi, Texas. I called her and she said, "Daddy, we would sure like you to come for a visit. We need a baby-sitter." Angela was just five years old at the time, and with both parents working, she had to go to different babysitters. Well, I packed up, told Emily not to let anyone know where I was, because the doctor had said not to let anyone know even the telephone number of where I was going to be.

When I got off the plane, the first thing I did was buy a big bottle of vodka. I was feeling very depressed and was planning to drown my sorrows. I had quit drinking in 1954 and joined

A.A. and hadn't had a drink since. Here it was 1970 and I was going to turn to it again.

I stayed there for a whole month. Angela was great company. She talked a lot and wanted me to take her places. We were busy all the time going to the beach, fishing, walking in parks. She was my doctor. Every time I would get the vodka out, she would come running to me saying, "What are you doing, Grandpa?" Well, I'd put the bottle away and we'd go out and do something. I never did have a drink of that vodka. That wonderful little girl changed my life that time. If it wasn't for Angela, and my wife, Emily, I believe I could have been dead.

4

AMBASSADOR OF GOODWILL

It Is Important to Promote Our Culture

I have always felt that it is important to promote our culture. I feel that my grandmother chose me to be a leader in this way. This is why she didn't want me to go to white man's school. She was afraid I'd forget about our ways; she wanted me to be a leader of our people, not only the Squamish people but of Indians from all over.

It was in the late forties that I first got involved in cultural things. The Coqualeetza Fellowship Club was the first Indian club organized in Vancouver. We wanted to put on Indian powwows in the summer where we would invite dancers and drummers from B.C. and other provinces. There was quite a bit of interest in the club. I remember how hard many of the women worked to raise money through the year so we could have the powwows. There was Mabel Stanley, Hattie Fergusson, Margaret White, Minnie Croft, Mrs. Kelly, who was Reverend Peter Kelly's wife, and Irene Rogers. Irene wasn't an Indian. We used to call her Sugar Irene because she owned the sugar factory. Irene Rogers was a great lady. She was very active in helping us. She was a widow. She had been married to Ernest Rogers of the Rogers sugar company family. So she helped us a lot with money, but mostly her time. We had quite a few white people helping us then. We had Charlie Collison, Mr. Noblet from the Bank of Montreal, Bell-Irving, an insurance agent. It didn't matter then. We all worked together, the Kwakiutl, the Haida, Cree, Tsimshian, and the white people. I always say, to get anything done we have to work together, even though we belong to different cultures. Katie Ferry (Adams) from Campbell River was also a member. She would come all the way from Campbell River to help raise money by putting on special dinners. She used to have the most colourful dancers. Katie and her children, they were wonderful, especially the little twins, her daughters. They all took part. I have a lot of respect for that family. We put on these banquets where we served traditional foods. After the dinner, we would put on a little entertainment. We charged about ten dollars. Lots of people still remember what we used to do. We also put powwows on at Ambleside, canoe races at English Bay. One time we had the canoe race at Stanley Park. That was the year that Sugar Irene donated a fifteen-hundred-dollar trophy for the winner of the canoe race. I don't remember who won but there were canoes there from the States, the Island. I remember that Willard Sparrow, from Musqueam, helped us a lot. He was a good promoter.

We got to be known as the group who had professional Indian dancers. We got invited to many different events that were going on in Vancouver.

I was the chairman so I got to go to everything with the women. People used to say things about me and "all my wives." Emily put up with it so I kept on because we were doing a good thing. We showed we cared about our culture and wanted other people to learn something of our ways.

Dominic Charlie was our elder at the time. I always say, "Go to your elders, speak to your elders, get everything." It just came natural to me because I was always doing promoting and I had Mathias Joe, Issac Jacob, Louis Miranda and Dominic Charlie. Dominic is the one recognized by many people as a medicine man. One time, when I got hurt, he came to see me. I had injured my leg. He said, "Okay, nephew." He always called me nephew. "I'll get you some medicine." Well, he did, and by god, within a week I was up and around. Another time I wasn't feeling well, he got some medicine; he boiled it. I never knew what it was. I didn't ask, but it cured me.

Dominic was the one who did a lot of talking. He knew I was going to be the leader so he'd come to me. A lot of times, we'd sing together. He knew a lot of songs and every song had a meaning. He gave me these songs. He said, "You learn it." He always told me, "A lot of things we do, we do in the summer, Simon, so as not to interfere with the *syéwen*, the Indian dancing of the longhouse."

Dominic was a person I could sit down and listen to. He always talked loud. I try to keep the good things in my head and I try to talk the way he did. So I keep telling the people, "Talk loud, you have a tongue, use your tongue, use your voice, so you can be heard." That's the way Dominic was. He loved to go around with us. We learned a lot of Indian ways from him.

I never forget one time when Dominic injured his foot. We thought he wouldn't be going with us to Harrison Hot Springs where we had been invited to entertain some people. They were big shots. We went to see Dominic Charlie, thinking he wouldn't be going with us because of his injured foot, but he was ready and raring to go. He forgot all about his aches and pains and was all excited about going with us. On the way to Harrison, we told him not to dance, just to sing. But he did dance the deer dance which was his specialty. I think of him today when I put on a show and I always get people to do the deer dance.

Dominic was from here, a Squamish Indian, who was loved by many people. He was married to my Aunt Josie. He passed away in 1960 at the age of seventy-six. We missed him very much at our gatherings.

The Coqualeetza Community Club changed its name to the Northwest Indian Cultural Association (NWICA). Our powwows were becoming a great tourist attraction. To start with we used to have one or two dance groups from Vancouver Island, like the Kwakwala from Alert Bay. Later we had even Americans at our gatherings. We would give prizes to those that had the best costumes or were the best dancers. As far as I can remember the Americans won most of the time because they always had the most beautiful costumes.

Sometimes, we would entertain at Brockton Point or we would go out of town to places like Nanaimo. We were so busy that sometimes I wondered when it was going to end. We planned shows, sports, dinners, and paid the performers who were invited to the gatherings. We even were invited to open Whistler Mountain. We entertained many people there.

All of the work we did for nothing; we didn't take any of the money we raised to pay ourselves. If we made a little money, we used it to organize another event. I think we all had great respect for our people and our culture and enjoyed performing our songs and dances for the public.

I was the chairman all the time the Northwest Indian Cultural Association was going. Hattie Fergusson was the secretary. She could type up a storm and sometimes she'd get mad at me for something and she'd type letters to me reaming me out. She wasn't afraid to say what she thought. This never interfered with our friendship, though. I remember when Hattie got very sick she asked me to come and see her. She wanted to ask me to give her a good Indian funeral. I said, "By god, Hattie, if I don't do it, I think you're going to haunt me." We had a great funeral for her; we did what she wanted.

The Northwest Indian Cultural Association gave me an award that I'm proud of. A group of women worked with me and we did a lot for the urban Indians. We had many functions such as arts and crafts shows, banquets. We even made medallions. I got a nice recognition from the Northwest Indian Cultural Association. They gave me and Emily a silver cup. It read, "Mr. & Mrs. Simon Baker, convenors and hosts 1963-64 Indian Days."

As well as being chairman of the NWICA, I formed the Capilano Indian Community Club for local events. The Capilano Indian Community Club put on the sports days and powwows which were held mostly at Homulcheson Park in Capilano. There's an interesting story about how Homulcheson Park got its name. Homulcheson is Squamish meaning "place where women and children fought and won." During the old days in the summertime, the men would go fishing. While they were gone the Haidas and Kwakiutl used to come down to raid for slaves. So they saw the canoes coming and the old people and the women and kids were the only ones there. Someone had the idea they should dress up like men and walk around the beach. When the Haidas and Kwakiutl saw them, they thought the men were still home and they turned back. That's how it got called Homulcheson, the place where the women, children and elders won without fighting.

The Capilano Indian Community Club began around 1942. I was the chairman and Emily was the treasurer. For the first few years we mainly put on Indian powwows. Our powwows included a sports day for children. We gave them ice cream, pop, hot dogs and other prizes. In the evening, people from all over came to see the Indian dancing. I remember by 1952, we were getting really big and about fifteen hundred were there to watch the show. From the Capilanos, the five main performers were Dominic Charlie, Issac Jacob, Mathias Joe, Dan Baker, my cousin, who did comic dances which people really got a kick out of, and August Jack, who was Chief Kahtsahlo.

August Jack Kahtsahlo was sort of a quiet person. He did a lot of hunting and fishing. He was tall, very tall and slim. He could walk. He used to take his wife, Mary Ann, across the ferry to the Union Steamship dock and put her on the boat to go up Squamish. Then he'd start walking. He had a trail up Lynn Creek. About three or four o'clock the boat used to land in Squamish and August would be there, waiting for Mary Ann. When you look at a map, it's not that far. People said he was like a mountain goat. He knew the trails. He went up Jervis, he went up Harrison Lake. Lots of people hired him to look for lost gold mines. That was what he did. He had a lot of knowledge of the area. He lived to be ninety-seven years old. He was quite a bit older than Mathias Joe, Dominic Charlie and Issac Jacob.

We got dancers from other places, too. That year Joseph Hillaire brought his dance group from the Lummi Reserve, which is close to Bellingham. They were called Children of the Setting Sun. There were about twenty dancers altogether wearing wonderful costumes and entertaining with their singing and dancing for about two hours. I remember that day like it was yesterday.

At these powwows, we usually ended up playing slahal, which is an Indian bone game. People crowded around to watch the players. I can say that the people who came to our powwows got their money's worth. Usually, everything was finished by 11:00 P.M.

I believe that the Capilano Indian Community Club did a lot to gain respect from the white people. The mayors usually came for a while and other dignitaries. The newspapers sometimes covered our powwows.

Our club did a lot of work because we had to get the grounds ready for the sports and powwow. It meant bulldozing, removing rocks in about three and a half acres of land. We had to put up a stage, a food pavilion, toilets. Everybody volunteered to help.

We tried to have a powwow every year and we tried to improve each year. We seeded the playground one year and made proper baseball and football fields. We believed in what we were doing and we helped other community clubs to get going. Our dream was to have a good community centre, with sports facilities and a few houses.

In 1953, we had a very special event. We applied to the B.C. Track and Field Association to put on a track meet at our community club grounds. I guess because of our good reputation for putting sports days and powwows on, we were approved. Many big-name athletes of that day came to the track meet from Seattle, Victoria, Kelowna, Vancouver and New Westminster. It was a great success, and of course everyone enjoyed the powwow show.

I remember announcing at one of our meetings with the B.C. Track and Field Association that I was looking for a long-distance Indian runner for the 1954 British Empire Games. I told them, "I have heard that there was an Indian trapper in the Skeena district who chased a moose for two days. The moose dropped dead and the Indian won. That's the type of boy we want."

It was always our hope to have our own Indian champion, a Capilano. I think if I didn't get injured playing lacrosse when I was in my thirties, I would have worked hard to be a sports champion.

Sometimes, our powwows were rained out. By 1954, we were having two- and three-day events. At this powwow, we had about four thousand visitors on the Sunday and only three hundred on Monday, because of a heavy rain.

Ellen Neel, an Indian carver from Alert Bay, carved a special trophy to be held by the person judged to be the best athlete each year at the Capilano Indian powwow.

I believe our annual track meets and powwows got bigger and better each year. It was getting known far and wide and the dancers, sometimes as many as five hundred, came from other parts of Canada and the States. By 1956, the Lions Club of North Vancouver was involved in getting the grounds ready. I liked to get not only our Indians involved but the white people as well. I was a member of the Lions Club so they knew me pretty well. I think about five thousand attended in 1956. We made British Empire Games sprinting star Mike Agostini an honorary chief of the Squamish. We named him Chief Tx̱̓'áy'usm (Lightning). We cleared about nine hundred dollars that year. We never made a lot of money but we were happy just to break even.

Our last big powwow put on by the Capilano Club was in 1958. This powwow was to be the biggest and the best. It was the longest as well because it was on for two weeks. I invited several tribes from Alberta to participate. That's the time when I got a peace pipe from Chief Ben Calf Robe. They made me an honorary chief here. They gave me the name of Chief Sunset. It was the Morley tribe, the Gleichen tribe and the Hobbema tribe that gave me that honorary chieftainship on the last Sunday before they left. They had a big ceremony and had food and everything. They gave me a prairie headdress, a beaded belt and a blanket and a song. It was the friendship dance song. We smoked the peace pipe. So I'm Chief Sunset. The sun was just setting when they gave me that name.

We had ten tepees in a beautiful setting. And they put on performances. For the first week, we were hardly getting any crowds because it was so hot. One of the newspaper men from the *Vancouver Sun* came over. He asked me, as chairman, "What's happening?" and I said, "I don't know." I said, "We advertised, we have a good show." He said, "I know, I watched and it's really something. I think a lot of people would be glad to see it." So he left and he wrote in the late edition. The headlines on the front page came out, which read, "Indians scalped by the gate," and he had a big write-up about our powwow, about all the beautiful and interesting things we had. The next three days the park was filled. So while the headline promoted some old ideas about our people, it worked. I was relieved. I was responsible because I had borrowed money from my company, Canadian Stevedoring, to pay the train fares of the Alberta people here and back for a total of over two thousand dollars. By god, I got my money back and some.

For nearly twenty years, many of us worked to keep our culture alive through the Coqualeetza Fellowship Club, the Northwest Indian Cultural Association and the Capilano Indian Community Club. My idea was to promote our culture, our traditions, our songs. I wanted to teach our people so they could teach their children, to know their identity, their grassroots. I want our people to have respect, pride and confidence. By leading the powwows, sports days, by being the chairman of the Indian cultural organizations and the master of ceremonies at the powwows, I wanted to demonstrate that if I could do it, they could do it.

Public-wise and tourist-wise, I knew we could also make a few dollars. I always feel that white people want us to participate in their celebrations. We are colourful in our traditional regalia. So we should participate. We can show the white people our ways, our customs, the beautiful things we create. As an emcee at powwows, I always explain everything, the different dancers, the costumes, the use of sweet grass so they can learn.

It's important for white people to come to our powwows and for us to go to their celebrations like the twenty-fourth of May parade. That way they can respect us and recognize us as neighbours. That we are not just Indians living on the reserve but that we could work together.

Elder Dominic Charlie, shown here in 1958 (George Diack/ *Vancouver Sun*)

Elder Issac Jacob at the Tomahawk Restaurant in North Vancouver

It's Our Country, So We Should Be Involved

The first World Exposition I went to was held in San Francisco in 1939. I was part of the lacrosse team, the North Shore Indians, that played an exhibition game there.

The Spokane World Fair was really good. The Indians had a longhouse there. I was involved with that from the very beginning. They approached me to find out how to have one built and had it shipped down to the States. Moses Antone and some of his boys did most of the work to build the longhouse. It was forty feet by sixty feet. I was longshoring so I didn't have much time to help, but I got all the equipment for them to use, like chain saws.

I went to the opening of the longhouse in Spokane. I really enjoyed it. They had a round area where the Indians danced and they had all the displays of arts and crafts.

I believe that Expo 67 in Montreal was one of the best expositions I attended. I was involved in it from the beginning too. I was one of the people invited to interview and select Indian girls from across Canada to act as hostesses at Expo 67. What a job it was to spend three weeks looking at fifty-seven beautiful girls! We had to choose five girls as hostesses and another five for backup. We tried to pick girls who really knew their Indian culture, since they would be meeting hundreds of people each day who would have many questions about Canada's Indian people. It was important that they know as much as possible about their people. The Indian pavilion showed the sad statistics and facts about our people.

The Indian people really made a showing at Expo 67. It was an Indian village where tribes across Canada could show their dances, arts, crafts, foods and tell their story.

I remember one day when the Treaty 7 people from Alberta were having a big gathering beside two tepees which had been put up. I was there with them dressed in full prairie Indian regalia. Suddenly, there was a great cloudburst like somebody made a hole in the sky. Within fifteen minutes, two inches of rain had fallen. The show had to be cancelled as there was water everywhere, not to mention the soaked costumes of the performers. My outfit was completely soaked, except for my headdress that I somehow found a place to keep dry. It took a couple of days for my outfit to dry. I accused the Alberta Indians of doing a rain dance. "It rains in B.C. but here it pours," I told them.

There were special luncheons put on for dignitaries. I got an invitation from Arthur Laing, the minister of Indian Affairs who was a friend of mine from B.C., to come to a luncheon.

While I was in Montreal, I was invited to Kahnawake, the Mohawk reserve on the outskirts of Montreal. They had a big parade at the cultural centre out there, so they got me on the float with a bunch of young lacrosse players. Then we went into their cultural centre and they had dancing and everything and I got up and said a few words. I got a very good reception there. There were lots of people from the Six Nations who remembered me.

Yes, I think the Indian involvement in Expo 67 went the right way. We were able to share our culture with the world in our own way. I think we should be involved in Expos if they are in our territory. It's our country. That's why the Mohawks got involved in Expo in Montreal in 1967. It is the satisfaction that we are recognized, the First Nations people.

The people all over the world should learn about us. They think we are all Apaches, Cherokees or Comanches because that's what they see on TV. They need to know we are many different nations, with different traditions, customs and languages. Expos give us a way to tell our story, who we are, how we live today. We need to educate our people and all the other people.

Expo 86 in Vancouver I felt was very tightly controlled, so I don't think we had a chance to show our true cultural beliefs. If I was in good health, I would have been more involved and we probably would have had something more. I was involved with the main organizer. I told him I would do everything I could but then I got sick and I couldn't. The results were disappointing because there was too much politics involved and too many people involved. The Indian pavilion had been planned as a joint venture between the Squamish and the Musqueam bands. A board of directors had been named, a model had been designed, and about $2 million had been committed. Plans fell apart when certain Indian bands were turned down for government funding for their band operations. They asked, "Why spend all that money on Expo when it's needed in other places?" They talked about boycotting Expo. This put a finish to the plans of an Indian pavilion at Expo 86. Later, when other funds had been found, I was asked to arrange to have the Musqueams involved in official functions at Expo such as the opening. Emily and I were invited to attend the official opening ceremonies.

The Musqueams performed their singing and dancing. Following the opening, I went up and thanked them. I told them, "I thank you guys for putting on a good show."

Ambassador for CP Air

I have travelled to many parts of the world during my lifetime. I enjoyed the many promotional tours I went on.

The first trip I took was in 1965 when I did a twelve-city promotional tour to West Germany for Canadian Pacific Airlines, Air Canada and the Canadian Government Travel Bureau. Jim McKeachie, a public relations director for western Canada based in Vancouver, asked me if I could go on a tour. He said he wanted to show people of other countries that Canada was a great country to visit. He explained that I could do performances in my Indian regalia in the different cities. I thought it would be a good way to educate people of other countries about Canadian Indians, so I agreed to do it.

I had known Jim McKeachie for a good number of years through lacrosse and through longshoring. His father and older brother had been longshoremen with Canadian Stevedoring and I was well known in the longshoring business. Jim came right to our house to ask me if I would be interested in doing some promotional tours for CP Air. I did six tours for them between 1965 and 1987.

Wherever I went, the people seemed interested in hearing about Canada, our tourist attractions, and they loved the stories about the Indians of Canada. I always wore my full regalia when I made my presentations, my buckskin outfit, feathered headdress, deer hooves. Sometimes I dressed prairie style and other times I wore my Coast Salish outfit decorated with paddles. Usually, I would speak in my language first. I'd say, "I welcome you people. I came from a faraway land. I travel like the big bird." Then I tell them in English that "I'm glad to meet you people from a foreign land. I'm glad to show you what us Indians wear for ceremonies and special events and what we do. I have a drum and I'm going to sing to you and I have a talking stick to tell you our story." Then I do the snake dance. They seemed to really enjoy the snake dance. Everybody wants to get hold of the snakes to see if they're real. I usually end my presentation by getting everyone to do the deer dance. The children had a lot of fun doing the deer dance that Dominic Charlie taught me. On these tours I spoke to the press, visited children's hospitals, clubs, schools, organizations. I was busy all the time but I enjoyed doing it. I think they could all tell that I was a very proud Indian and friendly too. I made a lot of friends on those trips.

That first tour in 1965 was a real experience. It took twenty-five days. They had me visit mayors of five West German cities. I gave each of them a souvenir totem pole to show friendship from our people.

I wrote home as often as I could to Mom, Faye and Charlie. The two youngest ones were the only ones still at home. I'd let them know where I was, how the trip was going, who I met, where I was staying. I remember complaining in one of my letters about the blankets. "These darn blankets, just can't get used to it. Only one cover like a huge comforter, either too hot and when the darn thing drops off the bed, you freeze. Oh well, no use complaining, nobody to listen to me." I don't know if they felt sorry for me or not. Maybe they thought it served me right leaving them behind.

First I went to Frankfurt, to Hannover, to Hamburg, to Cologne and on to Bonn and Berlin in Germany. It seemed there were always photographers and TV cameras around me wherever I went. Sometimes, as many as seven hundred people would come to my presentations. Once in a while someone would take me sightseeing but not very often.

I went to more cities, sixteen in all. They keep telling me, "Well, Chief, it's going to be quiet at the next little town, you can relax." Relax, my eye; they had more things for me to do at each stop. I never had much of a chance to relax in my room for even a couple of hours.

Following this tour, I got a letter from Dr. Gunn, who I knew from Vancouver. He spent a fair bit of time out here. I think he was an anthropologist from a university in Switzerland. He saw the publicity on me and wrote, "You certainly are an ambassador of goodwill, not only for the Canadian government but also for the good Indian people, who should be proud of your services."

In 1967, the Royal Canadian Air Force invited me to go to Marville, France, to dedicate and bless two twelve-foot totem poles. The totem poles were carved by my uncle, Chief Mathias Joe. I bought them off him for the Big Chief Drive-in Emily and I had up Squamish. We closed our drive-in so we had them up in our yard. When the RCAF wanted two totem poles, I showed them the ones I had and they said they would like to buy them. They were shipped to Marville. It was the No. 1 RCAF Fighter Wing stationed in Marville who bought the totem poles to be placed in Longuyon, France, and Virton, Belgium. This Canadian fighter wing was going to be moving to Lahr, Germany, and they wanted to show their appreciation to these French and Belgian people for their friendship to them while they were stationed there on NATO duty for six years.

Emily came with me. We flew in an RCAF plane from Trenton, Ontario, right to Marville, France. We had two ceremonies. The first day was in Longuyon, France, and the next day at Virton, Belgium. They weren't very far apart. I blessed the poles at both ceremonies and sang the totem pole song. The commanding officer had written to the Canadian government for about seven prairie-style Indian headdresses. He presented these to each head of a flying squadron.

After the ceremony we had to walk to the municipal hall where the reception was being held. People crowded around me all the way there. By the time we got there just about all the paddles from my regalia were gone. I guess they wanted a souvenir.

I have a nice picture where I'm sitting in a CF104 aircraft in my regalia. I wore my regalia a lot because everybody liked to see it, especially the children. Wherever I went, they would be following me. Jim McKeachie said I looked like the Pied Piper with sometimes fifty kids behind me.

While Emily and I were there, we stayed right on the base. They had to adopt me and make me a member of the Silver Foxes, so we could stay on the base. The officers gave us a big dinner and presented me with a certificate. It had written on it, "This is to certify that Chief Khot-La-Cha, chief of the Squamish Tribe, has been decreed an Honorary Member of H41 Squadron and is entitled to all rights and privileges accruing to a member of the Silver Foxes — 10 March 1967."

They showed us a good time. We were there for a whole week. We could go to their commissaries and buy things there. The prices were so low. Emily would get her hair done for sixty-five cents. Our meals were cheap. It was only about thirty-five or forty cents for breakfast.

On the trip Emily got lost one time in a crowd. She got pushed out. I had a hell of a time to find her, and oh, she got scared. After that she didn't want to go anywhere with me any more.

The best part of this was, when we had the Northwest Indian Cultural Association, we had a Bank of Montreal manager, Noblet, as our treasurer, and we had his partner there as our secretary. He was transferred to Europe. So Mr. Noblet, before he left, we gave him a good sendoff, a banquet and everything. Before he left, he shook hands with me and said, "If you ever come to Europe, Chief, you come and visit me." I never thought I would ever get to Europe. When we were at Marville, we went to the bank to change our money. We were going to go to Paris to spend a few days there. When I looked up, I saw the Bank of Montreal. The first thing that hit me was Noblet. So I asked the young guy, "Do you happen to know a Mr. Noblet?" "Yeah," he says, "that's our boss." "Where is he?" I asked. "Oh, he's in Paris," he replied. So I said, "You phone him and tell him that the chief is here." He did, and I got on the phone to Noblet. He said, "My god, Chief, what are you doing over here?" I said,

"I've come to take France over and I want to have a meeting with you." He said, "I have to leave tomorrow to tour the banks in Europe, but you come over here early, I'll have everything set up for you. I'll have my staff take you out on a tour all through Paris." That's what they did. They picked us up at eight in the morning and brought us back by five. Before we left there, the guy said, "The boss said if you need any money, you are to let us know." I looked at Emily. She said, "No, we're okay." On the tour, they took us to the old Vimy Ridge where the First World War was fought and all over Paris. I told Emily, "We never would have seen so much without these people." That was a good trip for us. Emily could see the kind of things I did, how the people treated us.

In 1968, I made another tour in Germany for CP Air. I was there for four weeks and I went to twenty-two cities. I had a special invitation to go to Lahr. I was met there by a group of Germans dressed in full prairie Indian regalia with beautiful headdresses. I was surprised that the officers had an Indian club. They adopted the name Winnebago-Sioux. They knew a lot about Indians, mostly learned from books. They made me an honorary chief. It was the first time I was made an honorary chief and I had to go all the way to Germany to get it!

I was very busy every day for four weeks, going from city to city visiting CP Air offices, going to schools, hospitals, malls. Everyone wanted to see the Chief. I put on the same show many times. The children especially wanted to meet me. I made sure I said a few words and shook hands with them. When I got home, I sent a letter and a picture to one of the little boys I had met. He wrote back to me. "Dear Chief Choti-la-cha: Thank you very much for beautiful letter and the picture. My friends opened their eyes in surprise, as I showed the letter them. When I come to Canada one day, I will visit you. In my special science projekt about the Indians I got a very good grade. When you came to Munich again, please visit us, than I will show it to you. In my free time I like to play Indians. Then I go to the wood and make a little tepee for me. But most of the white children can not play realy good Indians. I would be very glad if your grandchildren would be here or I could go to them. I am sure, they can teach me more, than I'm learning out of books. Do you have an eleven years old grandson? Would you please ask him to write to me? Tell my greeting to him. Love from your little brother Jens."

CP Air sponsored me again in 1972 to Madrid, Spain, where they were officially opening their travel agency. It was a big celebration. I put on my performance. They seemed to enjoy my presentation just like the Germans did.

I went to a bullfight. I always remember two little boys who were watching me and imitating everything I did, all my actions, every move I made. I had fun watching them from the corner of my eye because I really didn't like watching the bullfight.

In June 1980, CP Air had their twenty-fifth anniversary of the polar route from Vancouver to Amsterdam in Holland. The first pilot that flew the polar route was there. I presented two large plaques to CP Air, which I believe are there at Schiphol Airport in Amsterdam. One was of the Thunderbird and the other was the Killer Whale. I gave the airport manager a talking stick. I was only there one night on that trip.

In 1981 CP Air flew me to Birmingham, England. It was to publicize CP's shipping of a large cast iron pipe elbow for BC Hydro. It was to be used in a hydro-electric project. They gave me a half-inch steel peace pipe and other gifts. As usual, I visited a number of schools, children's hospitals, shopping centres, to tell of our culture and to promote Canadian tourism.

My last promotional tour was to Hawaii in June 1987 for Canadian Airlines, which used to be CP Air. Faye, my youngest daughter, went with me to help me out. I got Len George and his family to come with us to help with the performances. We were to perform at the Third Annual Festival of the Pacific in Honolulu.

Faye knew I had travelled all over the world many times entertaining people so she thought I knew everything, and now she was all of a sudden to become a high-profile Indian, too. She was in a panic trying to figure out what she should take to wear. Mother had wonderful handmade Indian clothes and jewellery, but she was about a size eight and Faye about a size twelve. So Mother got busy and made Faye a most beautiful Indian outfit. Just like when the kids were young, Mother still has that great gift to sew whatever is needed.

The day we were to leave, Faye's husband, Billy, and their children came to pick me up to take us to the airport. I had my talking stick, drums, snakes, my outfits. The kids unloaded the van at the airport and soon we were on our way. Just as we were taking off, Faye remembered not seeing my prairie Indian headdress on the luggage ramp. She realized we had left it in the back of the van. Well, there was no use worrying about it. I told her I had my Coast Salish headband packed and I would use that.

Len George, his wife and sons enjoyed the flight with us. We got to Honolulu at 10:30 P.M. We were greeted by all kinds of people representing Canadian Airlines International, the Festival of the Pacific and other companies. We were taken to the beautiful first-class Hilton Hotel.

Our agenda consisted of four performances during that week. Two were at six-thirty at night and two at noon. Faye was very nervous about the first performance. People think she's quite outgoing. Mother always says, "You're just like your father," but standing on a stage in front of an audience that evening, she wasn't too sure about that. She was to do the introductions of Leonard and his dance troupe and me. Well, I guess she takes after me after all. Leonard's wife, Sue, knew Faye was nervous, and she said Faye looked as cool as a cucumber up on the stage.

The next day we went on a sightseeing tour of the island in the morning and in the afternoon I had an appointment with the governor of Hawaii. We went to the state capital and actually sat in the governor's office. It was very impressive. We met with the governor's aide and we presented him with a hand-carved paddle.

Before we knew it our trip was coming to an end and it was time to head home. It seemed like we had been away for three weeks instead of five days. We crammed so much into such a little time and everything was a new experience for Faye. Faye said on our flight home, "I learned so much just watching you, getting to know Len and his family, and what the responsibility and rewards are when you are an ambassador for your own people." We enjoyed the time the two of us spent together alone. Faye is very close to both Mother and me and she has always done things with just Mom. This was the first time for just Daddy and Faye.

When we got home Faye told the family, "It doesn't matter how many times I see him perform and entertain people, I still enjoy watching, and it seems to me I learn something new every time. It makes me feel very proud that I was lucky enough to have him for a father. I know some people say to me, 'Well, Faye, maybe you could follow in your dad's footsteps,' but I think those are pretty big shoes to fill. Somehow I don't think of myself as a Ms. Khot-La-Cha."

Faye calls this trip her "Aloha with Daddy." I think it's important that she had this experience. I was proud of her, too. She was a beautiful Indian maiden and she spoke proudly about our people and our culture.

It was the first time I had worked with Len and his family. I knew his father, Chief Dan George, very well. I can see that Len is like his father, and his sons and nephew are learning the Indian ways. Len is an ambassador of his people now. He's young and can continue the job.

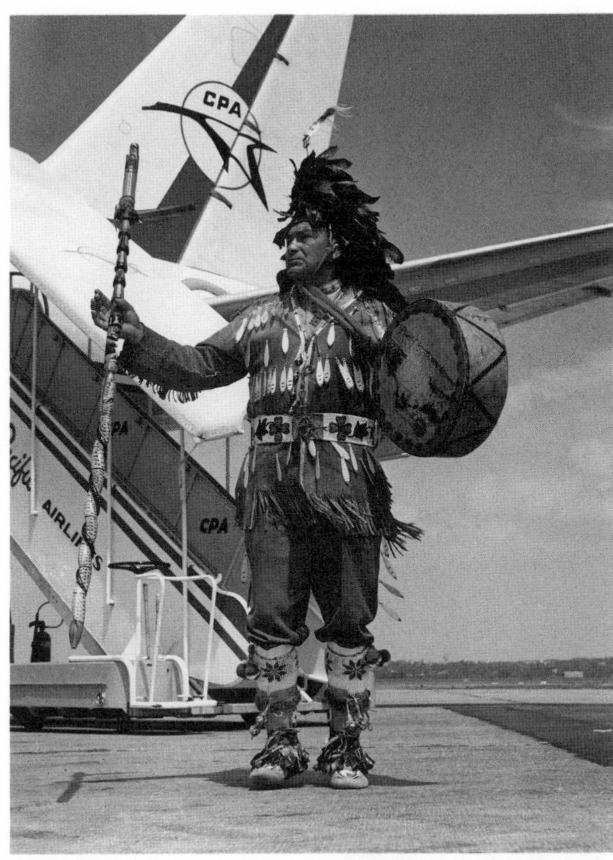

Leaving on first tour of Germany for CP Air, 1965 (courtesy CP Air)

With CP Air travel agents in Germany, 1965

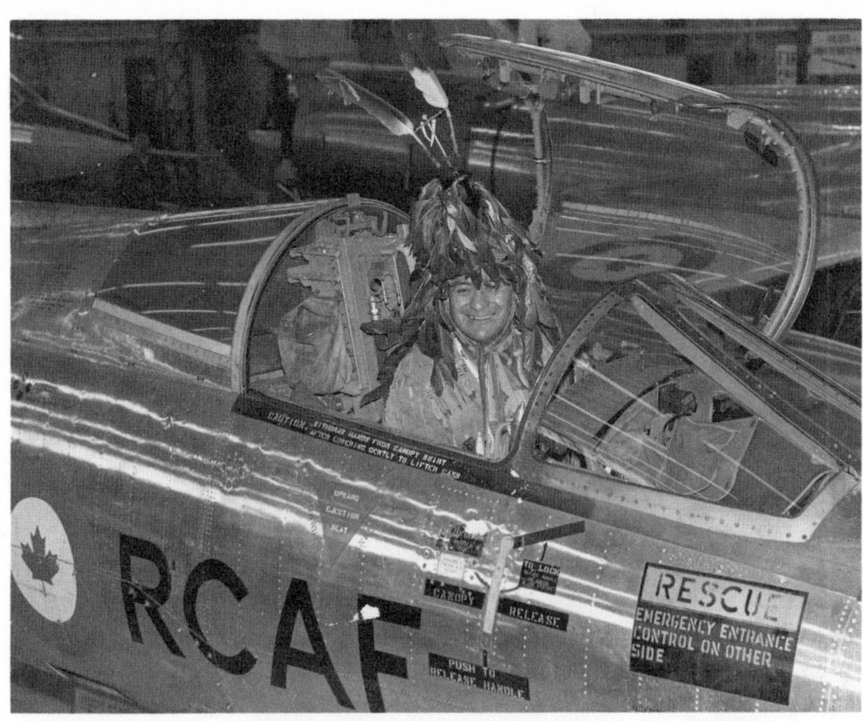

In cockpit of RCAF fighter plane in Marville, France, in 1967

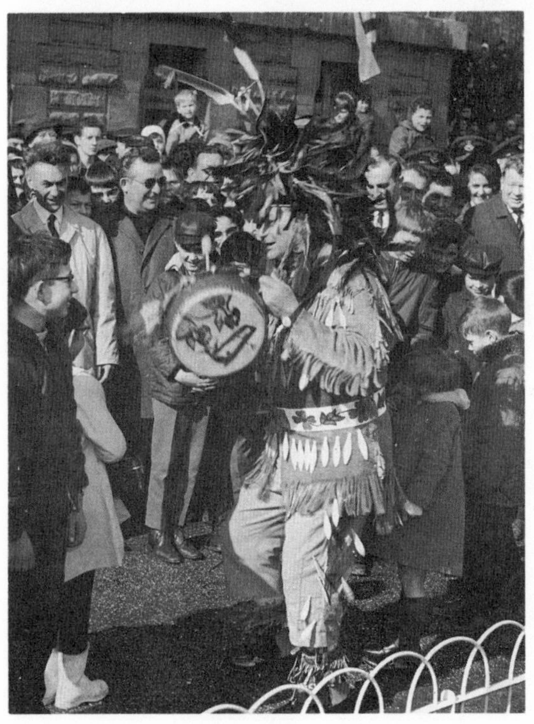

Doing a friendship dance at a totem pole raising in Longuyon, France, in 1967

Visiting the Japanese

I had a good name with CP Air with all the promotion I did for them. It was through them I was invited to Kobe, Japan, in 1981 to perform at the opening of the new Kobe port. They asked me to bring a group over. I got John and Robert Davidson and Gary Edenshaw. They're Haidas. I got Gail Sparrow from Musqueam and there was my niece Brenda Baker and myself.

The Japanese paid for our trip, five different groups, big companies.

The port was on a new island some twenty to twenty-five miles long that they took twenty-five years to build. The way they built that island, they had a conveyor belt twenty-somewhat miles long to a big mountain. They had it going day and night.

They had a real beautiful set-up there. They had an open pavilion with seats right around the platform. It was covered, but it was open. People could come in and if they didn't like the show they could just wander out again. When we put on our show there, someone was telling me, "Chief, that's the first time people have come and stayed and watched." When we came to the last farewell, we introduced our gambling game, the slahal game. I don't know what the interpreter told them, but you should have seen what happened! They all started throwing money in. At the end of the performance there was lots of money there. So we said we would donate the money to the crippled children's hospital. What followed was a front-page picture of our group telling how we had donated the money to a good cause. We were getting paid anyway, so it didn't matter to us. But they said it was the most wonderful thing that had happened. I told Gary Edenshaw, "That's what you call promotion." He said, "I know, Si, I'm learning a lot from you." We did the deer dance and the slahal song. Most of the time, people like those in Japan don't understand the dances. So I told Gary, "I'll explain what the dances mean, so I think we'll do some other dances." We did four other dances.

As part of our visit we went to many other areas and performed at big shopping centres, the children's hospital and the opening of a big complex built by B.C. Lumber. They had built new houses. The houses weren't very big, because Japanese don't have big homes, but they were nice compartments. That was quite an experience for me because I had a lot of experience longshoring and lumbering. I met quite a few B.C. men there that were in the lumber business.

On the last day, at the airport, they gave us the money that was left over from the sponsors. We each got seven hundred-somewhat dollars. That was good pay for seven days' work, and a chance to show the Japanese our culture.

After we got back home, I got an invitation from Wendy Sparrow (Grant), "Come over, Chief, our people want you." They were putting on a big do at the Musqueam Community Hall. There were Japanese visitors from Kobe. They were the ones we went to perform for. To honour the Japanese, the Musqueam put on a mock Japanese wedding. I think Robin Sparrow was the bride. I forgot who was the groom. It was beautiful and the Japanese liked it.

The Musqueam people had the do to thank me for organizing the tour to Japan. I felt very good. It was like meeting a long lost brother, everyone was so friendly.

I believe I introduced many people around the world to the Coast Salish and other Indian people in Canada. They seemed to have very little knowledge about us. Many times I was asked, "Do you live in a tepee? Do you scalp people? Do you use a tomahawk?" I always tried to set them straight on these questions. They were interested in hearing what I had to say. They always seemed happy to meet a real Indian chief.

I have received many letters from children and adults from all over the world thanking me for visiting them and telling them about our people here in Canada. I believe that many of the children that saw me years ago still remember me. They will be grown up now.

I always say, "You have to be proud of who you are." I am a proud Squamish Indian. I can hold my head up and speak loud about our people. It helps to have a sense of humour, too, so I always joke and try to make people feel at ease.

The Sechelt people said I was "an ambassador of my own culture and of the human spirit." That's how I try to live.

New Zealand: Kia Ora

I always say it's good medicine to me to go out and meet people. I enjoy travelling. One place that I'm very happy that I got to was New Zealand. It is probably the furthest place I've gone, some eight thousand miles from Vancouver, and I went there three times. I really love the Maori people of New Zealand. They seem to have a very similar culture to us Northwest Coast Indians in Canada. They have canoes, the long kind with many paddles; they have carvings, their use of the cane is the same as our talking stick, and they eat a lot of seafood like we do. I have heard a story repeated many times that many, many years ago several canoes of Indian people left Bella Coola, a village up the northwest coast of B.C. No one knew where they went. It is believed that they sailed from island to island and found people already settled on the islands until they reached New Zealand. This is where they settled. The Maoris talk about their ancestors arriving in nine canoes in Aotearoa (New Zealand). It's quite possible that the Maoris originated here in the Northwest Coast. They sure look like us B.C. Indians.

When you go to New Zealand, you soon learn some Maori language, like *Kia Ora*, which is a greeting. There are about three hundred thousand Maoris in New Zealand. They are working hard to revive their language and many *pakeha*, or white people, now use common Maori words with their English. It was an eye opener to learn how strong the Maoris are in their language and culture. Their cultural centres are called maraes. This is where they gather together for meetings, funerals or celebrations. They also hold classes for children called the Te Kohanga Reo, or Maori language nests. I enjoyed visiting these language centres and hearing little children speaking in their native language. Whenever I go to these centres or schools I always talk to the kids. I talk to them in my Squamish language first so they can hear how it sounds. Then I tell them in English where I come from and how we live. No matter where I go in the world, children and sometimes even adults ask if we live in tepees and hunt buffalo. I like to help them to learn, so I take time to explain that we have many different kinds of Indians in Canada and that each group have different languages, songs and dances.

I sing a few songs and do the deer dance. They have fun when I get them up to dance.

On some maraes, they have adult classes where they learn different skills and crafts. They do a lot to try to help the youth gangs to learn a trade and their culture. It seems they are involved the same way we are to try to have self-government, to get their land back. I learned a lot of things by going there three times.

My First Trip

The first trip I made to New Zealand was in January 1977. How I got involved was really something. I was invited by the MRA, Moral Re-Armament. They came to the house. There was four of them, and they brought Chief Walking Buffalo with them. I invited my uncle Chief Mathias Joe, Dominic Charlie and my brother Bill. They came here. We had quite a meeting at my home, to hear such great speakers and what they were trying to do for the people in this world of ours. They were more or less working with people who were having a lot of problems. This MRA organized a conference in New Zealand. They brought a man from New Zealand to come here. I was interested and I wanted to go to the conference.

When we arrived in Auckland, there were already quite a few there from Alberta. They had their headdresses and whole costumes on. I had my headdress, beaded jacket, talking stick, masks, snakes in my duffel bag. The customs guys took all my masks and asked me a bunch of questions. I was getting quite offended, and I told one of them, I said, "You watch out, the Great Spirit is watching you; something is going to happen to you because you're interfering with all this. This is very sacred to me and all my people." Anyway, they put everything away to fumigate it and hold it for twenty-four hours. I had to go back the next day to get it. Well, you know what happened? The next day they had the worst electrical storm they have ever had in Auckland. I said to myself, "What a coincidence!" The custom guys must have wondered if it had anything to do with what I said.

We stayed in the area of Auckland and went to a marae. Another group came from Yakima, Washington. They travelled with us for only two or three days. There were a lot of young people in their group, so with that bunch and the ones from Alberta we made a very colourful entrance. I wore my split feather headdress, my Squamish regalia. I was the last speaker on the last day. The conference was about all working together as brothers and sisters to try to solve internal and world problems. The theme was "Partnership of Nations to Build a Better World." I told them that Indian children must be taught the old ways to preserve our culture and heritage. I said, "You have to give your words, your will, your heart to people to make them understand. Our ways have changed. Now we are going back to them." I spoke in my language. I talked about my talking stick. After that, we went to other maraes and the Alberta people told me to speak first. So everywhere we went I did most of the speaking.

There was a group there called the Song of Asia who put on quite a performance. It was a cultural production of many native songs and dances. There were people in it from all over, Canada, Fiji, Asia, New Zealand, you name it. That's where I met Lee Crowchild from Alberta. He was just a young man. I met Te Rangi, too, who was a young man at the time.

I knew his father. Later Lee Crowchild married Te Rangi's sister Aroha.

I paid my own way to New Zealand that time. It was worth every cent. The conference was important. The principles of the MRA are in the tradition of our people from away back. We have to work together to solve problems to make our lives better. I always say, "If the attitude doesn't change, the mind doesn't want to work with the people." That's the lesson for all of us.

After the conference, we went to a sheep ranch. We were invited to a *hangi* for a big feast. It was the most beautiful meal I ever had. I never liked lamb or mutton, but over there, it was delicious — maybe because it was cooked in the ground for several hours. They showed us how they shear sheep. They do it very fast. Some of our young boys tried and managed but weren't very fast.

So the MRA was about helping people that were suffering, the treatment they get from the government, the treatment they get from losing their identity, their culture. It seemed to spread. Many people joined the MRA. I think they are going stronger today.

The trip was a good one. I went as a member of the Squamish Nation. I met a lot of wonderful Maori people. I always remember Naudie Audie. She took me to Bastion Point where they were having a demonstration because they were fighting for their land. There were thousands of people there, about a hundred elders. They said, "Chief, you speak." So I talked about our sacred land, and no way the government was going to take it away. I spoke of our culture, how it is related to the land. My talk was cultural, not political.

Naudie Audie worked for social welfare. They all came down to the airport when we were leaving. She got hats and bags from everybody and she was collecting these for the chief to take home as souvenirs. I'm glad I got involved then with MRA. They still keep in touch with me.

My Second Trip

I'm always willing to go back to New Zealand. In 1988, the First Nations House of Learning at the University of British Columbia was planning a tour of New Zealand. Verna Kirkness, the director, had visited there in 1986 and was very impressed with the Te Kohanga Reo, the Maori language renewal program for children from birth to five years. She advertised for thirty people who wanted to join the tour to visit the language centres. We had a good group. Some were from Ontario, Manitoba, Saskatchewan, Alberta, and most were from B.C. There were both Indians and non-Indians. We even had three teen-agers with us. My son Ronnie came on this trip with me. I was glad to have him along to take care of me.

When we arrived in Auckland, there was quite a number of Maoris there to greet us. They took us to a large room at the airport to welcome us. It is a tradition of the Maoris to press noses. This is to join the minds together. On that trip, we visited many maraes, heading first up to the northern part of New Zealand. Then we headed west till we got to Wellington, the capital of New Zealand.

At every marae, we had the traditional welcome. You can't just walk onto a marae, you have to be given a proper welcome. One of their people comes out to meet you at the edge of the courtyard. Each marae has a courtyard, then someone at the marae, usually a woman, calls you onto the marae. The one that came to meet you calls and tells them that we are friends coming in peace. We move on a few yards at a time and the two, the hosts and visitors, exchange words. Finally, when we are close enough, speeches begin. Several Maori men speak to us in Maori. They are telling us of their ancestors and that we are welcome. After each speaker, they sing a song. Oh, the Maoris have the most wonderful voices. After their speeches are finished, then it's the visitor's turn to speak. I was the main speaker for the group. Usually three would speak, all men. That's their custom. I would speak in Squamish first, telling them we are glad to be there, where we are from, why we are there. Then others would speak. After the last speaker, I'd sing a Squamish song. I tried to teach our group the song so they could help me out.

We would then put out our *koha*, which is a token payment for our stay on the marae. When one of the Maoris comes to pick it up, we are officially guests of the marae. Then we line up and go and press noses and hug one another. Usually after this we eat. The Maoris are like us in eating, too. They put out a big feast every time. After that we can come and go on that marae. They are very spiritual people. They pray before meals. They have evening and morning prayers. When you leave a marae after a visit, you have a farewell ceremony. Again there are speeches and exchanges of gifts. So we followed this protocol at all the maraes we visited. We travelled by bus from place to place.

The scenery was beautiful. It was quite a bit like B.C. We visited many language centres, schools and business ventures they have. The time went by fast even though we were there for about two weeks.

That trip I needed a rest. I was happy to be there with Ronnie and all of the others. I enjoyed going to the South Island as a tourist, visiting Queenstown, visiting all the maraes, and meeting some people I met before and many new people was wonderful. I remember the boat ride and coming back in the evening and getting together, giving each other presents to remember each other. It was well planned. I said to myself, "I give thanks to the Great Spirit; I give thanks to you people who invited me along."

I think the visit to the parliament where a women stood up and thanked me for what I did eleven years before was a highlight. I didn't think anyone would remember, but I guess what I said about our land, our relationship to our sacred land, stuck with her. I was quite honoured to be mentioned in the New Zealand House of Parliament.

The most exciting was in the North Island when we went to visit one of the Maori schools and I was introduced. A little fellow shouted out, "MacGyver, MacGyver!" I guess he had seen me on a show on TV where I was acting with MacGyver. The kids got very excited and had a lot of questions to ask.

I got a lot of pleasure out of travelling with that wonderful group of charming people. We travelled many miles, met a lot of good people, learned how our friends down under do things. We were all very impressed and very tired as we headed back home.

My Third Trip

I was very fortunate to go to New Zealand once more in December 1990. The House of Learning at U.B.C. was organizing a group to go to the second World Conference on Education of Indigenous People in New Zealand. They invited me to go with them to be their elder and speaker. They said they would have a young man along to look after me because none of my boys could come with me this time. Sure enough, a young fella, Bill, who was a student at U.B.C., was always around to look after me, carry my bags and help me find the washroom.

I never have to worry when I go anywhere with that bunch from U.B.C. As an elder, all those who travelled with us took good care of me. They made sure I was comfortable. I didn't have to worry about anything from the time I left home.

I never thought I'd go to New Zealand three times in my life. Ever since my first trip in 1977, I met and I got to know a lot of Maoris. When we had the first World Indigenous Conference on Education here in Vancouver in 1987, I really enjoyed meeting the large group that came here. I believe there were a hundred that came and about thirty of them were elders. One even came in a wheelchair.

That first conference was put on by the First Nations House of Learning at U.B.C. We were asked if the first day of the conference could be held at our longhouse here in Capilano. Our people, the Squamish, were proud to host that first day. I always remember how packed the longhouse was as two thousand people from seventeen countries tried to get in for the official welcome by our Squamish elders and chiefs. We were organized. Those that came from furthest away were seated first. I welcomed the visitors from around the world to Xwmelch'sten, the Squamish territory. Then Chief Joe Mathias and others from other countries spoke and our Squamish singers and dancers performed and gifts were presented to the head person of each country from the Squamish.

Then everyone went outside to learn in a traditional way. There was a spiritual tent for elders. It was packed all day. I think those who went in in the morning never came out.

I guess this shows that elders' teaching is important to many people. Some watched song and dance performances on a large stage. There was a tent for the traditional games, one for plays and one for traditional food preparation.

All this time, my boys and others were barbequing salmon over a thirty-foot pit they made. People were standing around watching them clean the fish and putting it on the pit. Of course, we had a big feast to end the day. It was a good time and I believe everybody enjoyed themselves. The Maoris were a big hit. They are very outgoing and friendly, and since there were one hundred of them, they stood out. Everywhere they went, they were singing with their beautiful voices.

In February 1988, we handed over the sacred trust of the World Conference on Education of Indigenous People to the Maoris. We had a big gathering at the Musqueam hall with delicious traditional foods cooked by the Musqueam. Sir John Bennett, chairman of the Te Kohanga Reo Trust, and Anna Jones of the Te Kohanga Reo staff, along with the Kahurangi Cultural Group, came to accept the sacred trust.

We had a great evening of songs, speeches, gift giving. The First Nations House of Learning gave the Maori delegation a talking stick and a drum as symbols of trust.

So, since we hosted them on our territory, I wanted to go to the next conference.

When we arrived in Auckland, we were taken over to a Maori school for an official welcome which included a big feast. Even though we had travelled by plane for about fourteen hours, we all had a good time meeting old and new friends.

From there, we went to Honi Watiti marae in Auckland. For the next week we travelled by bus to Gisborne, stopping at maraes along the way. The scenery was beautiful and we were glad to have Mike, a Maori, as our driver again. He was one of our drivers on our 1988 trip. We went to one marae high up in the mountains on that west coast. It must have been very hard to drive there because it was steep and very narrow. On our trip to the airport before we left, I gave Mike a Squamish name: *x̱wúx̱wse'l'ḵn*, which means mountain goat. We had a little ceremony on the bus and I put my Squamish headband on him. You should have seen the strange looks he was getting from other drivers and people in cars beside us.

Every marae we went to, we had the greatest hospitality. We always had the welcome and farewell ceremonies. It was like we knew the people all our lives.

The conference was held at the Queen's marae in Ngaruawhia Turangawaewae Marae, near Hamilton. I met the Maori Queen in 1977, in 1988 and again this time. She's a great lady, very gracious and friendly. She had a reception for us one evening. One of the young boys from our group was selected to attend. He got all dressed up. I asked him if he wanted to meet the Queen. He said yes, so I took him over to her and we had a little chat.

Our group was chosen on the opening day to lead the procession. There were so many people there that the procession was about half a mile long. It was a good conference. Every day, there were workshops. Our bunch participated in them. I didn't attend any sessions because it was difficult for me to sit on the ground. The workshops were in large tents and people sat on the ground. There was a lot of discussion on language and culture and I understand that they were very interesting.

It was a fine gathering. When you get all the indigenous nations together, it is really something. It is important to think of what we want to do in the future for the children to know who they are, their language and culture. Every evening, there was wonderful cultural performances on a very large barge. That first day, the procession ended near that barge where a ceremony was held. The Maori hosts and special guests were on the barge, which served as a stage. Several long canoes paddled by the barge giving a salute to the people. It was wonderful looking from the barge to see all the hundreds of people sitting on the shore.

Several groups put on dances. When it came to Canada's turn, Te Rangi, an old friend, asked me to emcee that part. Well, we had a lot of performers, because not only our group was there but many others. Anyway, I put on as many as I could and asked each one to do a short performance. Everybody co-operated and it went well.

There was so much that happened at that conference and on that trip that I can't remember it all. The main thing is, we had a chance to meet each other, indigenous people from around the world, to share our stories, our beliefs, to try to improve the education of our children.

I thanked the Great Spirit for caring for me, for the privilege of travelling and meeting people, for sharing our teaching, what our ancestors taught us.

As for the Maoris, they are like my brothers and sisters. I love their golden voices and all their beautiful songs. They have a strong spiritual belief in the Creator. I hope I see them again.

The Pied Piper leads a group of children in Sydney, Australia, in 1977

With Sir John Bennett, chairman of the Te Kohanga Reo Trust, at a gathering in Musqueam in 1988 (Arro Photography)

On our second trip to New Zealand, 1989. *Left to right*: Rudy Leon, Corry Archibald, Shirley Norris, Cathy Hall, me, Judy Marchand, Ron Baker, Jo-ann Archibald

My Acting Career

I always believed that Indians should act the part of Indians in movies. The late Chief Dan George did a lot to open the doors to acting. I never miss watching the television series *North of 60* because it is about our people and acted by some of our own great talents.

Around 1988 and 1989, I was asked to act in a couple of episodes of *MacGyver*. In one episode I was cast as Uncle Len, a Native trapper who, along with my two nephews, saves MacGyver from Sasquatch. The Sasquatch was a thief in disguise who had killed a man and kidnapped his daughter to get their boat. MacGyver, of course, was trying to capture the Sasquatch and rescue the girl. They were in the midst of a tussle when I, as Uncle Len, and my nephews arrived on the scene. After saving MacGyver, I tell him a legend about Sasquatch's wife which I had heard many times as a boy. Sasquatch's wife came down in the evening where children were playing in the night and she'd grab those that were playing after dark. She'd put these two or three children on her back in a bag. She'd take them away up in the mountain, where nobody even attempted to go, because they knew in their hearts they wouldn't dare go into the territory of the Sasquatch. But when his wife took these children up there she would make them dance around the fire, and if they didn't, they would be punished, or they did something to the children. That's why our parents told us this story time and time again as we grew up. We really believed this. So as soon as it got dark, we were gone home, off to bed.

In another episode, "The Mask of the Wolf," I played the role of a grandfather called Two-Eagle. Two-Eagle had buried the mask of the wolf, a very sacred mask, in a secret place. It was his peoples' custom to seal or bury very precious things. Only his grandson knew where the mask was buried as he had been with his grandfather when Two-Eagle had sung a song as he buried the mask. When the grandson was an adult, he was kidnapped by a group who had learned about the mask and its value. Again, MacGyver saves the day and the grandson is rescued.

I also played a part in a documentary called *The Traveller.* The traveller is the story of a man who was retracing his life as the husband of an Indian woman. He had returned to white society but felt he had to live his experiences over again. In the documentary, I pick up the traveller in my truck, drive him down a logging road. As we drive along, we overtake a large logging truck. I couldn't get by him and I say, "You think you own the road."

It was quite an experience going to an area about forty-five miles north of Squamish to do the filming and seeing how much that area had been logged. It looked like somebody went through there and stripped the mountainside. I can understand why our people are fighting about clear-cuts. Our people wouldn't think of doing something like that. I would support keeping most of the forest the way it is. It takes seventy-five to a hundred years to get back a forest. It's a long time to wait. To cut a two-hundred- or three-hundred-year-old tree down is something.

The parts I played in these three shows were very short, but I found the length of time it took to tape even a thirty-second clip could take an hour or more. As usual, I enjoyed this experience. I was nearly eighty years old when I played these parts so I would say my acting career was very interesting but tiring.

Though I only acted in these three shows, I have had people tell me they saw me on *MacGyver.* I was very surprised when the Maori schoolchildren in New Zealand recognized me from *MacGyver*. You could tell they were proud to meet me.

It is good for our children to see us in movies and on TV or in books. It is the new way of telling our stories or showing that we can be whatever we want to be. We just have to believe in ourselves.

Thank You for the Recognition

I believe the greatest distinction that anyone can receive is to be recognized as part of the community, the nation of Indian people, the reserves, and also the non-Indian society. I belong to several clubs. I take part in many things with organizations, schools, universities, conferences, meetings. I like to help people. I have done a lot of fund-raising for projects over the years.

I have been involved in one thing and another for the last sixty years. I guess it's by association for many years that I have been chosen to get quite a few recognitions. I have a rumpus room in my basement where I keep all my plaques, certificates, trophies, drums and other gifts that I have been given. The room is pretty big and it's full. I like to sit down there and enjoy what has been presented to me. I like to read the letters from all over, even Europe and New Zealand, that people wrote thanking me for my performance or talk or any other kind of help. People appreciate it when you try to help.

When people ask me about my awards, I say, "Come and visit. Come and see my rumpus room." They are usually surprised to see all I have. I guess people know I collect baseball caps. I have so many, I had to put two lines of wire from one wall to another so I could hang them up. This past winter, I had a carpenter come and build more shelves and cupboards in my rumpus room so I could keep things more in order.

I appreciate all the recognitions I got from everybody. I want to talk about just a few of them, because if I try to talk about all of them, I'll need two or three books.

The Native Brotherhood of B.C.

I believe the award that I really was most proud to receive was an honorary lifetime membership from our own first organization in British Columbia. The Native Brotherhood formed in 1933. It was at their fiftieth anniversary in 1983 that five of us received this great recognition. There was Guy Williams, Eddie Nahanne, Frank Calder, Clarence Joe and myself. We were each given a gold pin. This is something I really cherish. I wear it everywhere I go; I wear it as a symbol of the development of our own organization that has had to struggle to succeed in helping our people.

When I first got involved in the Brotherhood, I was quite young. I sat and listened to some of the great leaders of that day, Ambrose Reid, Bill Scow, Reverend Peter Kelly, Andy Paull. They were all good men.

I associated with Andy a lot when I was playing lacrosse and even before then. He was the manager and coach of the North Shore Indians lacrosse team for many years. He always got me involved. He'd say, "Come on, Simon, you're the biggest man we got, the youngest." I got involved in all kinds of sports with him. I played baseball, canoe pulling, and I even helped him canvass for money for lacrosse. That's how I learned how Andy worked, how he talked to people. He was respected by many people. So going with Andy, a lot of the people later recognized me when I had to go around canvassing for money for our powwows. I worked like Andy worked.

I used to go with him and my uncle Mathias Joe, the two leaders. They always asked me to go with them. Andy had a personality that I always admired, the way he carried himself. He was a man who educated himself. He was a great speaker. He could sit with the most intelligent people, judges and everything, and Andy could speak. He knew the Indian Act right through and he used to associate with the old group that first started. They were called the Allied Indians.

One time, they called me to go to a Native Brotherhood meeting in Prince Rupert with them where all the big guns were meeting. There was Ambrose Reid, Kelly Adams. There were about five of them. To see Andy in action and to see all those other leaders speaking about land and all the other things they were fighting for! The big problem at that time was the different groups, the Haidas, the Tsimshian, the Nisga'a, the Coast Salish were all talking about their rights, the fishing and hunting, but they weren't working together. I admired Andy. He could make them sit down and listen and think of how to work together to solve the problems.

I always respected Andy. He had that personality, dedicated to his church, and he wanted to beat the white man at his own game — go to court. Andy went to court many times to defend people. He wasn't a lawyer, so he always said he was an interpreter.

Andy was about twelve years older than me. He was a very good model for me.

The Brotherhood was into fighting for the rights of the North Coast fishermen. That was how the Brotherhood formed from the Queen Charlotte Islands, the Nass River, the Skeena River, all the way down to Alert Bay. It took quite a while before they got down to Cape Mudge.

The Brotherhood did accomplish a lot. They fought to get medicine and the vote for the Indians of B.C. They fought to have Indians allowed to buy liquor in the liquor stores and to be able to go into beer parlours. Each of the five presidents — Guy Williams, Bill Scow, Dan Assu, Robert Clifton and Ed Newman — did accomplish something. We had members of our own here with the Native Brotherhood for a few years. Eddie Nahanne was the business manager for quite a few years and Tim Moody was the secretary. Our Squamish people were involved. I got involved going to their conferences and meetings. I co-ordinated their banquets, or put on a show for them, or was an emcee or even a bouncer.

The Native Brotherhood was independent. They never got money from the government to run the Brotherhood. Guy Williams, the first president, always stressed that point. They charged every fisherman so much in dues; the captains of the seine boats had to pay much more than the crew. They had a lot of money to keep their administration going.

United Native Nations

It was an honour to receive recognition from the United Native Nations. They invited me to a conference as one of the spokesmen. I received a framed certificate from the United Native Nations on the theme "Working Together for Our Children." It is a Certificate of Honour which reads, "This Certificate is presented to Simon Baker by the United Native Nations Society in recognition of the contribution you have made to the Aboriginal Rights Fight and the building of a better place in British Columbia Society for all Native Indian Peoples. — Bob Warren, President, UNN Society, January 22, 1982, VIC [Vancouver Indian Centre], Vancouver, B.C."

I told the people when they organized the UBCIC, the Union of B.C. Indian Chiefs, that they should recognize the non-status Indians. They didn't want to recognize people who didn't belong to reserves. I kept telling them, "We're all the same. Our fathers and mothers married out but our father or mother is an Indian from birth. They came from the Indian side and I can't see why we should separate our people. We are all fighting for the same thing."

The UNN formed as an organization that would include the non-status Indians. It is changing across Canada now. It should be that we recognize everyone who has Indian blood in them. This land belongs to all of us. If it wasn't for our forefathers, the white people would not have been able to make the trip across Canada. It was the Indian guide who helped these people travel across Canada. That is why many of our people married into the white race. They had children who were called half-breeds. Then the French Canadians came and that was the bunch that created the Metis group. Then there are the non-status. I'm status so I live on the reserve. They're not so they don't live on the reserve. And the only difference there is we're registered and they're not.

Sechelt Nation

In 1985, the Sechelt people made me an Honorary Chief. There was a special meeting that time at Sechelt. They were signing a historic agreement on self-government.

The late Clarence Joe was a great friend and colleague of mine. Somehow, I always felt like one of the Sechelt members. Clarence and I always worked together. When he was the band manager, he always invited me to go with him, whether it was Ottawa or somewhere else. He told me, "Si, I always like to take you with me because you are well known; everybody recognizes you!" Whenever we would go to the Parliament Buildings in Ottawa, to visit Senator Guy Williams, we would be invited to the parliamentary restaurant for dinner. We'd go in there, and before long the minister of Indian Affairs and other ministers would come and sit at our table. It was quite surprising the kinds of questions these M.P.s would ask us, Clarence and I. We were in Ottawa trying to get some answers to resolutions that had been given by our people to government. We wanted to know why we didn't get any answers. We wanted to try to get some results to some of the issues. They would say, "We never got any letters," and I'd say, "Well, who got them?" I guess the secretary or somebody at a lower level. That's why we always say, when we go to Ottawa, we go to the top banana. We get the straight answers. We want to know why the resolution has been sitting on a desk for six months, sometimes a year. We followed up on a very important resolution about a surrender, where we wanted to develop our land. By god, they turned around and went right after the party. We said we want an answer in two weeks. That's how Clarence and I used to work. Go right to the top. A lot of our people used to say, "What do you guys do? How do you get in?" It is not how we got in. It's how those people came to us, you know. Sitting there in the parliamentary restaurant with all these big people. Clarence did most of the talking. He wasn't backward. Clarence was fighting for a lot of things, the same as us. I had a lot to do with

Sechelt. Sechelt respected me. When Clarence died, the children kept saying, "By god, we should do something. The Chief here, let's give him an honour," so they put on a big dinner for me, invited the high school kids that time when they gave me that honour. I was the most proud person when they gave me that recognition. I can go to Sechelt any day and I could stay anywhere, with the Joe family.

So, to be recognized by the younger people, Chief Stan Dixon and the councillors, was a great honour. Stan was my son Red's good friend. So, I have known Stan for a long time. He still comes to visit me quite often to discuss what he's doing.

They gave me a beautiful plaque when they made me an Honorary Chief. They called me an ambassador of goodwill. I always try to promote my culture and to acknowledge our human spirit.

Recognition by Non-Indians

I always try to work with all people. The non-Indians invite me many times to go to their celebrations, meetings, conferences, you name it. They appreciate it when I go and help them out. Most of the time, I dress up in my regalia and promote our culture with good humour. I remember one time, many years ago, when we had a big do in Vancouver with canoe races, track and field meet. It was in 1958, the B.C. Centennial Year. The government gave me a bronze dollar with an inscription, "British Columbia 1858-1958. Mr. Simon Baker of B.C., Centennial Award of Merit." British Columbia joined Confederation in 1871. In 1971, I was given a certificate of merit "for [my] distinctive contribution to the British Columbia Centennial Celebration marking 100 years of the start of the Canadian Confederation."

Every year on July 1, they have a big parade in North Vancouver sponsored by the North Shore Lions Club. I participate in the parade every year. I am the grand marshall of the parade. I lead the parade. During this last parade, they didn't pick me up. So the parade was on when I got there. An old police car was coming up. The guy hollered, "Hey stop," and I jumped in the rear and everybody was getting a great kick out of me sitting in an old police car with my headdress. I usually ride right in front in a convertible. I'm now an honorary member of the North Shore Lions Club. I told them I sometimes wasn't feeling well and wouldn't be able to attend all the meetings. They didn't want to lose my membership so they gave me an honorary membership. So I participate in the parade every year and I go to the Lions Gate Hospital where they have a great big cake for all the patients on their July anniversary. I go there with my headdress, with the mounted police and the mayors of both the city and the municipality and some other dignitaries. It is quite a deal. I missed it this year. I hear people were asking, "What happened to the Chief?" Somebody said, "I guess he's gone, left the country." So they miss me when I don't show up.

I'm also an Honorary Beaver. The Capilano Beaver Colony are the Boy Scouts of this area. Two of my boys, Peter and Ronnie, joined when they were boys. So I was involved with the Capilano Beaver Colony for a number of years. Every year, they had a gathering, a campfire, with a lot of ceremony. Many groups of Boy Scouts would gather together. Each group had an Indian name. I would go there in my regalia to talk to them and sing them a song. One year they made me an honorary member. There was quite a few Indian boys in the Beaver Colony. I had a beaver carved for me from a guy up Squamish. He used a chain saw. I gave it to the Beaver Scouts. They put it on wheels because it was quite heavy and they would pull it in whenever they had meetings. It was a good thing for all those young kids. I was also made an honorary member of the Boy Scouts of America at Sooke on Vancouver Island. Over fifteen thousand Scouts came from all over the world. They gave me one of their crests.

University of British Columbia

I always stress education, ever since they told me that my grandfather went to England in 1906 to ask for four things: hunting and fishing rights, land and education. Education was the one thing he wanted for his people. That seemed to always follow me, and I wanted my children and everybody else's children to get an education. Any grants available, I'd say to my children, "Go and get it, get all the education you can because that's what we need for our people. That's the ammunition of our future generation to fight the government for our rights. We have to be able to read between the lines, the great words that lawyers, governments use. To do this, we need education."

My daughter Faye worked for NITEP (Native Indian Teacher Education Program) in North Vancouver for quite a few years. She would invite me to come once in a while to their centre at Norgate School. I always remember this one time, I went over when all the students were gathering at North Vancouver. They were from NITEP centres in Kamloops and Chilliwack and other places, and all the students and the workers from U.B.C. were there. I believe it was an orientation for NITEP students from all the centres. The North Vancouver centre was hosting the gathering. That's the time I met an old friend that I had not seen for over ten years. Her name was Verna Kirkness, and she was the new head of the NITEP. I first met Verna in Ottawa in 1970. She was a young Cree woman from Manitoba who was very interested in culture. We were attending the First National Indian Cultural Conference organized by Dr. Ahab Spence, who was working for the government then.

Well, I was very happy to see her again and to know she was working in Vancouver. Verna began to invite me to U.B.C. for different gatherings. I got to meet the students and had a chance to get acquainted with them. What impressed me about NITEP was that there were many mothers and even grandmothers who were going to university to be teachers. I think it's good for the youngsters to have mothers and grandmothers studying with them. NITEP opened the door for our people. That's why I love to go there every year to graduation. So, from then on, I have been a U.B.C. elder, helping whichever way I can.

In 1986, I was made an honorary NITEP graduate. I was glad to receive this honour. It reminded me of what I've been striving for all along — education for our people. I think to myself, "Now it's working, the things that we tried to negotiate for. In the old days, everything was hard. You couldn't get anywhere. They'd push you around. But finally, there are many good people involved in education. Now we can get somewhere."

The year I was given the NITEP award was the year that my own granddaughter, Angela, Nancy's daughter, graduated from the Native Indian Teacher Education Program at the University of British Columbia with a B.Ed. I was very proud of Angela. We did everything to help her in her studies, as far as our culture and heritage. Anything that I had that she wanted for her classes or practice teaching I let her have to learn about our culture. I knew Angela was going to make a great teacher.

At that time, the NITEP centre at U.B.C. campus was in one of the old wartime huts. It was renovated, and though it was old, it was a place for our students to gather. We had many potluck lunches, meetings, parties there. Sometimes it was very crowded, especially when other students like the law students would come over for a special gathering.

One time, Verna told us that she got a memo saying that in two or three years the old huts were going to be torn down. The students, staff and us elders, Vince Stogan from Musqueam, Minnie Croft from Haida Gwaii and myself, talked about what we should do to have a place at U.B.C. The idea to build a longhouse came up.

After that, many meetings were held to talk about our plans, especially after Jack Bell donated a million dollars to be used for First Nations at U.B.C. That was in March 1989. Everybody agreed this would be the start of the fund for the longhouse.

I always remember all of us interviewing three architects who had done some buildings, like schools and a longhouse project in Prince Rupert. The architect for the building in Prince Rupert offered to fly Verna there to see the building. Verna told them she wanted an elder to go with her. So I went. We flew up in the morning with the architect and came back that evening. The Haida-style longhouse looked really great. We took pictures to show the group at U.B.C.

We had two or three meetings with each architect and we decided to pick Larry McFarland. He had built the Prince Rupert longhouse. It wasn't only for that reason he was chosen, but we all liked his manner. We wanted someone who would listen to us, because we wanted to say how it would look, what kind of rooms we need, like a library, daycare, great hall, student and elders' lounges, offices for NITEP, Health Care, Law and the House of Learning.

The House of Learning started up in 1987. It wasn't a real house; it was in an old hut near NITEP. Verna was the director of the House of Learning. Since 1987, they tried to get more Indian students to get into other things like medicine, forestry. The House of Learning was in charge of the longhouse planning.

Once we picked the architect and had the first million dollars, the students, staff and us elders met quite often in 1989 to 1993 when the longhouse was finished, and we had a big celebration in May 1993. About two thousand people came to the grand opening.

That longhouse was put there for our children and our children's children. We, Indian people, made all the decisions about it. I remember when we had a bus to go around U.B.C. campus to look at five different places we could put the longhouse. We decided on a spot that would be near the centre of the big campus. It had to be where students could easily drop in for lunch, coffee, meeting, to work in the computer room or library. We picked a good spot.

The only thing was that it wasn't near the water. That's when I brought up the problem. I was born and raised by the river. Water is very important. Our old people used to say, "Water is your best friend." They would tell us to go and swim even when we were just toddlers. Mother Earth gave us water and we were taught, "Where did the water come from?" It comes from the mountains, the snow. "Where did the water go?" It went out to the sea. It goes in a cycle. If we didn't have water we would perish. I felt, why couldn't we have a waterfall by the longhouse? Everybody agreed with me and we told the architect what we wanted and it was put in. Today, a lot of people tell me they enjoy the waterfall. They know water gives you a new life, a good feeling. Water is the most important thing in our lives.

I remember that once we said what we wanted for our longhouse, size and everything, we needed a building of 2043 square metres. We needed between $4 and $5 million. We had a million from Jack Bell with matching dollars from the province. We still had to get about $3 million.

I know Dr. Strangway, the president, and Dr. Birch, the vice-president, and others at U.B.C. worked hard to find the money. I tried hard too, to get some money.

Every time I went to some kind of meeting, small group or big group, I'd go after money for the longhouse. I remember a big meeting I was invited to in Whistler. There must have been about two hundred there from all over Canada. At that banquet that night they had big round tables. There were about eight people at each table. When I got up to entertain, I told them about the longhouse we were building at U.B.C. I said to them, "All of you sitting there, pick someone from your table to be the head of your table. I want each of you to donate to the longhouse. Give your money to the person at your table that you picked to be the head. Then they can bring the money up. I'm going to entertain you now. If I get a lot of money, I'll entertain all night." Well, by god, they donated pretty near fourteen hundred dollars.

Then I went to another meeting in town. There was only twelve people. I asked them to donate to the longhouse. I believe I got fifty dollars. So that's what I did at all the meetings I went. I figure I raised about four or five thousand dollars.

There were two other big donors to the longhouse. They were Bill and June Bellman, and James Bertram and Ilse Wallace. All the big donors got Indian names. Emily and I gave Mr. and Mrs. Bellman their name. We named them Whei Wha. It means "echo." We picked that because Bellman was in radio and TV broadcasting and echo is like sending messages.

It is a good feeling to go to the longhouse. Whenever I go there, students always come and talk to me. I ask them, "Who's your father, or your grandfather?" I usually know them because I travelled all over B.C. One day a young man came over to me. He told me his grandfather was Johnny Clifton.

Well, I knew Johnny. I knew all them Cliftons. It was good to see a third generation going to U.B.C.

We have an Elders Room where we can visit with students. I donated a portrait, a painting of myself, to the students. They put it in the Elders Room. I tell them they should have pictures of all the elders there, like Minnie and Vincent. We were the elders that did a lot of work to get that longhouse built.

Now that it's built, there will be more students coming to U.B.C., young and old. I read in the last longhouse newsletter that they are gonna try to have a thousand students by the Year 2000. It will happen. Maybe I won't be here, but it's gonna happen. More of our reserves are going to take on self-government and that's the thing — we need educated administrators, developers, doctors, you name it.

In 1990, U.B.C. gave me a great honour. They gave me an honorary doctorate of laws. It was a great experience in front of all the people, getting such an honour. Now I'm Dr. Chief Simon Baker. I go to all the graduations now. They put the cap and gown on me and I walk with the president and others up to the stage. I believe it's good for the Indian students to see an elder up on the platform.

I believe it has been a good experience, to work with all the good Indian and non-Indian people at U.B.C. I want our Squamish people to make use of it, because I had a hand in that longhouse being there.

I always try to tell people about the things I did in the past to work with my people, work with other people, Indian, non-Indian. In anything that was going on, I was always asked to take part to be the co-ordinator. I have the knowledge and experience to do many things. I know how to carry myself in a committee meeting or in a big crowd. I'm never backward. I'm always talking to people. They ask me a lot of questions. They always seem to like my answers, and my name is picked out for awards. That's one thing I didn't realize when I was working, I wasn't trying to get some big thing out of it.

I always remember what my grandmother said to me: "Son, someday you're going to be a rich man, not in money, but in friends."

I always entertain people with a lot of good humour. I can be involved in anything, sports, culture. I learned everything.

I get a call and someone says, "You've won this award." I just say, "Thank you, thank you for the recognition."

Us elders, we appreciate recognition. It gives us something to show our children, our grandchildren and other people.

I get letters, phone calls from all across Canada, to tell me when people die.

With the Brock House Society Senior Award, which I received in 1993, I opened the door for other First Nations elders to be recognized for the contributions they make to their communities. I was the first Indian to get it. There will be many others in the future. As Clarence Joe and I always said, "It's important to get your foot in the door!"

I should turn my rumpus room downstairs into a museum so people can see all the gifts I received during my travels and my participation in different functions. I have many ball caps, drums, talking sticks, paintings, books. You name it; I got it.

Chief Simon Baker, Honorary Doctor of Laws, University of British Columbia, 1990, and Verna J. Kirkness, Honorary Doctor of Humane Letters, Mount Saint Vincent University, 1990

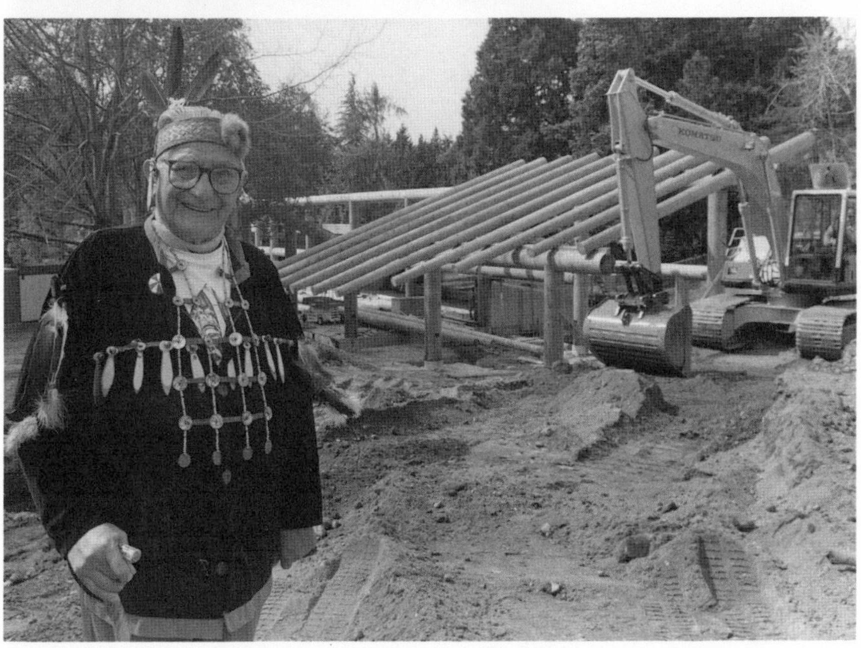

The U.B.C. First Nations Longhouse under construction in 1992 (Gavin Wilson)

Leading a healing circle in front of the Squamish Recreation Centre, 1993 (Nick Didlick/*Vancouver Sun*)

5

ELDERS SPEAK WITH GREAT HONOUR

Keeping Our Traditional Ways

When I was a boy I used to enjoy listening to the words of wisdom, the philosophy of the Indian people. It was highly regarded by many. They gave advice, support and encouragement to the people who were in sorrow, in trouble. Our elders always spoke very well in their own languages. Today, very few people know their languages. When we do speak our languages there are hardly any people in any gathering who understand what we are saying, so we speak in English so they can all understand what we are trying to present to them. Elders speak with great honour, which is difficult to put into English. This is why I say the words of our elders must be cherished.

Our people believed in the Great Spirit. They performed the animal dances because it was the animals that really helped them survive in the old days. They got the fire, the meat, the seafood, the beautiful trees. That is why I sing the totem pole song that refers to the mountains, the trees, the snow, the gift of water; the tree gave us the house, the canoe, the cedar bark. That's what that totem pole is all about — giving thanks. It's our spiritual things that we believe in. The carvings on the totem pole are symbols, reminders of our connection with nature. In a way, it's our bible, our record. We don't pray to the totem pole just as people don't pray to the Bible. It is simply our record.

An elder always feels great when people come and talk to you. I always tell people it doesn't hurt to come and shake hands and say, "I'm so and so, the daughter of, or the son of. . ." This is what I cherish most in life: meeting and shaking hands. I practise it all the time. Whenever I go to a big do, I get asked to speak. That's quite an honour. I'm always ready. I'm never stuck for words. Somehow, it seems to come naturally. I've lived a good life in the Indian way.

You know that us elders always believe in keeping our traditional ways. By forming an elders group, we are trying to get a program. We are trying to get some direction in how we can be helpful to the young people. That is why the potlatch is important. People are saying today, "I have to get my family recognized, I have to leave something to my children to remember." It takes commitment, time and money to pass on our culture. I always say, "We don't want to take it with us." The memorial potlatch held by my sister Amy and her daughter Betty in Comox accomplished something that the young generation can understand. They brought something back that their forefathers practised.

It was important for Emily and I to go to this potlatch. We arrived there at 1:00 P.M. They were just preparing food in the hall near the longhouse. A marriage ceremony was also going to be held. They had the woman dressed in her button blanket. The family all sat near the doorway and they had their elders there. They had to convince the elder of the bride's side that the groom was worthy and they had to make him laugh. There were about five different groups. The first group got up and spoke in the Kwakiutl language. The parents said, "No, you haven't got enough." Then the next group would go up telling about what the groom could do, what kind of person he was. Finally, the last group got up and told jokes. They made the elder happy. They had to get through him to accept the man. The bride-to-be also smiled. So that was a sign that they accepted him. When that was done, the couple went out to get ready and they started the dance. The man had to perform all kinds of different dances. The last group of dancers had cedar bark cloaks on them. An elder spoke and brought the man and woman together as husband and wife. I didn't understand what they were saying in the Kwakiutl language, but I knew they were giving advice, giving encouragement. The Indian philosophy is something expressed in speeches. After it was over, he kissed the bride, and they sat back and watched the completion of the marriage ceremony, which took about three hours. Indian time is used, which means we take all the time we need. The older people sat as witnesses. These two had been married quite a few years in the church. So what was done at the potlatch was extra. Many of the young generation was there and now understand what it's all about. I think it was a good demonstration of reviving the old culture, the old ways. There aren't many of these, but they may be coming back.

After the wedding ceremony, we all went to the hall for dinner. There was more than enough to feed the four to five hundred guests. They had salmon, rice, soup, potatoes, bread, bannock, dessert. It wasn't overdone but everyone had enough. I had plenty! We were there for about one and a half hours. Then we went to the longhouse. A dance group of boys did the Hamatsa dance and the Kwakiutl dance.

The highlight was the Hamatsa, the Wild Man dance, when the young men came out and hollered. There were about twenty young boys, hollering with their squeaky voices. They danced just like the old-timers. Several young girls did the blanket dances. We were the last to dance, the whole family. I put on the ermine hat, blanket, and danced with the others. I danced with Ed Newman, just the two of us before the family came on. That was a real honour for me to dance with Ed. I told Ed not to watch my feet; I might confuse him because I have my own fancy step, I'm used to dancing my own way. The most important thing about dancing is to keep time with the drum. Emily got up many times to dance. At first she was scared to, but I told her not to be. So I was very proud of her.

My sister Amy and her daughter Betty spent two years planning for this potlatch. When they started to plan my sister asked me what she should do. I told them, "Go and see the Kwakiutl elders." So they went to Alert Bay to talk to elders. My sister had married a Kwakiutl and she, of course, was Squamish, but she wanted to honour and remember him in his culture. They made all kinds of things to give away. They knitted and crocheted cushions and tablecloths. They spent more than ten thousand dollars for blankets, cups, plates, you name it. It took about an hour to distribute the truckload of gifts they had to give away. The gifts were in laundry baskets. They gave them to the elders first. Everybody got something and most people got several things, basket loads. They were also passing out oranges and apples. They gave money to the men who were speaking while the gifts were being given out. Two dollars each. Earlier they had given ten dollars each to several people who were to be the main witnesses. After it was finished, people gathered their gifts. What they did was what the people appreciated. The younger people were admired for attempting a potlatch since Betty, my niece, did a lot of the planning. It took two years and all that money. Many people got up and spoke and thanked the young people for putting on the potlatch. Betty was helped by other people her age.

The memorial potlatch was put on by my sister Amy for her late husband, Sam, and her son Sam Jr. Sam Jr. was just a young boy, twelve or thirteen, when he went out fishing and drowned. So, the two Sams died. She had their picture up. They gave James, her oldest son, a name, his grandfather Sam's Indian name. That's what the family wanted. He became a chief; his grandfather was a big man. When James spoke in the end, they gave him a standing ovation. He danced and spoke like an old-timer. People who didn't know him thought he must have danced a long time. But I knew he hadn't. It was as if it was just in him, and he began to dance. He knew he had to do it. This is what he was telling the people in his speech.

That is why they wanted the potlatch, to pay the people for the memory of her husband and son. Sam Jr. died six or seven years ago. Sam Sr. died quite a long time ago.

When I spoke, I said, "We're all related now, because everyone of the family is married to someone from the West Coast. One is married in Alert Bay, in Kingcome Inlet, another to a Haida. We're all related!" This reminder made people happy because at one time it was very difficult, people were divided, the Tsimshian were there, the Haidas were there, the Kwakiutl were there, the Cape Mudge were there. Now we are all mixed. The children are part Haida, part Squamish, or part Kwakiutl and Squamish. That interested the young people.

When the evening ended, Betty said she was nervous right to the last night. But everything went beautifully, so I said, "You better give thanks to the Creator. Your father, your grandfather, your brother was there with you." That's the way we believe. The elders that were there, not many left still alive, came to shake my hand. I kidded them and asked, "Does your mother know you're out tonight?" We had a good laugh.

In order for me to keep the teachings of our elders, I had to keep coming home. After I left school, I had to accept the things that my grandmothers keep reminding me of, my grassroots. I tried to practise what they taught me, keeping up my culture from the teaching of my elders. I was glad to listen, to obey and practise our way. I still have the knowledge, wisdom and philosophies of our elders. I had to keep learning my own culture, my language. Going to the outside was like going to a different world.

It's very difficult at my age to teach my grandchildren to pass on our culture to future generations. I'm very happy when my grandchildren ask me to go to their schools to put on a performance. I'm glad to do it because all the children enjoy it. The parents even phone or write to thank me for going to that school, to demonstrate our culture and our heritage. I can do it because I believe in it. I was raised in it, brought up with it. I didn't have to go to school to learn what I'm trying to give the kids. I'm not telling them anything that doesn't belong to us. It's there; it's ours. That's why I'm really proud to talk about our way.

The kids want to learn all about us, how we used to live, how we live today, what we believe. This was the same wherever I went — Germany, New Zealand, England, you name it.

Our people, especially elders who are able, should be speaking in schools every day. When I go to schools I have my regalia. I tell them about my headdress, my paddles, designs. I take my talking stick and explain all the symbols on it. I talk to them about totem poles, potlatches. I tell them legends. I say some words in Squamish language. I like to keep them interested, so I let them come up to hold my talking stick while I sing a song with my drum, and while I explain the talking stick, someone can look after my drum. They love that. I always make them do the deer dance.

In our culture, the talking stick is an important symbol. It is held by the chief, the host or the head of the house. On the talking stick, each family has their own crest, legend and stories of their family.

I carved my own talking stick quite a few years ago. It has been all over the world with me. It's about five feet long. I explain every part of it. Starting at the top, I have a Thunderbird which represents the Great Spirit. He is the creator of the world. He's the one that created lightning, thunder, rain and wind. As he sat up there and waved his wings, he brought wind. When he flashed his eyes, lightning would strike.

Then I have our crest, the Bear crest, which is part of the Coast Salish Nation. We are told that in the beginning, when the first two people came, these two people had their firstborn child. They had quite a hard time to survive. The Bear family came and adopted the baby and raised the baby. They taught the baby how to survive with nature and its surroundings. The baby grew up and returned to our people. That is why our people respect the Bear.

The third symbol on the talking stick is the Killer Whale. The Killer Whale, sometimes called the Black Fish, are people from the sea. My grandmother told us we were members of the whale family. She would go out into the inlet fishing every day to talk to the whales as they travelled north.

The fourth symbol is the two-headed Sea Serpent. Our people were very afraid of the evil spirit which is represented by the Sea Serpent. One day a young warrior was given a vision on how to kill the two-headed Sea Serpent that threatened our people. He went away up Indian Arm, off Burrard Inlet, and trained himself to dive in this deep cove every day so that it would give his body power to stay longer underwater. He was told what tools he had to gather when the day came when he had to kill the two-headed Sea Serpent. He made a lot of sharp sticks, and pitch with mud. That day when the snake came, he was ready. When the snake opened his mouth, he threw the sticks and pitch into his mouth so that he couldn't close his mouth. He did the same thing to the other side of his head. A bone connected the two bodies together. Finally, the snake choked and sank to the bottom of the lake. The young warrior had to wait a year before the body would decompose so he could get the bone. After many weeks of diving, he succeeded in getting the bone. After he got the bone, he received great power. When he returned to our people, it was as a medicine man.

On the talking stick, there are four symbols to represent our belief that everything in Mother Nature comes in fours. It is painted in four colours that we live with. Black is for the sea, red for the sun, green that covers our mountains and trees, and blue is for the sky, rivers and lakes. Finally, we have four cycles in our lives, which are birth, naming of the child turning into adulthood, marriage and death.

This is the story of my people that I carved on my talking stick.

It is very important for children to learn about us so they can respect our people. I feel very happy performing for children. I know that somebody is there behind me, coaching me. I believe it is a spiritual program that I've practised from a way back.

Much is taught of our culture in the school now from kindergarten right to teen-age. They learn dances of our culture and other cultures in Canada. Today, our doors are open. We accept others and we talk, ask questions, and mostly they're happy when they leave. They enjoy our foods. We give them good hospitality. That's how it is with our people.

My cousin Lawrence Baker teaches the Squamish language and culture to our kids in North Vancouver schools. Just recently, I gave him two traditional Squamish songs. These songs were passed down in my family, and I learned them from my uncle Chief Mathias Joe and elders Dominic Charlie, August Jack and Issac Jacob.

These men said to me, "Simon, we'll teach you the songs and we want you to learn them and we want you to pass them on. Pass them on to your children so that their children will learn."

The two songs I gave Lawrence were the Welcome Song and the Totem Pole Song. The Welcome Song was sung by my grandfather, Chief Joe Capilano, to King Edward VII in England in 1906, to thank the king for hearing the brief the Native leaders had brought to him. The Totem Pole Song was sung to King George V by Chief Mathias Joe. I said to Lawrence, "Now I have the honour and pleasure to give you these songs for the use of our people. Tell them to use it in the proper way and don't criticize, don't argue. Learn the songs and be proud that somebody is there to teach you. I would like you people, you young generation, when I give you these songs, use it for yourselves. Don't ever record it and start selling it. This is for our own use. But when you go to a big celebration, use it. If you have to use that song to raise money, you go ahead, but you make sure nobody records these songs whenever they are sung anywhere. In the Totem Pole Song, we pray to the Great Spirit. We're thanking the Great Spirit; we're thanking Mother Earth for everything that's provided for us. Respect Mother Earth and it will take care of you, and that's what it's all about."

The way of our old people is coming back. This whole land, this country was bare with hardly any people. Now, the community is building so high that we are squeezed to a point where we have to accept their ways and they have to accept our ways. That's what it's coming down to. Today, we tell our children, "You go to school; you learn their ways. You come home; you learn our ways. We've got the drum, a lot of stories." It has benefited my children, especially my grandchildren. Three of them went through university. When they came to me to ask about our ways, they have the full knowledge of what I've given them.

Every time, when I get up in the morning, I say a little prayer. Now I'm at the age where today is one day for me. I don't know how long I'm going to be here. When tomorrow is gone, the full cycle of my life is complete. At my age, I'm eighty-three now.

I always say when you live to be a hundred you've gone through the four cycles. I feel so good — about harmony.

Mother Earth provides, shares. We respect Mother Earth. Everything that we have today, our clothes, our food, all the beautiful things, we thank the Great Spirit for the wonderful day. There are a lot of bad things in the history of yesterday that we'd like to forget. Growing up, going to school, marriage, our work, everything. There have been a lot of dull days, hard days.

It is important to teach the good things, not the bad things. I never say to people, "Oh, go away, I'm not feeling good." I just see them or I phone them to arrange for a different day.

Our old people had their stories, their teachings. They had their flood, their Adam and Eve, all those things. Adam and Eve were adopted by the Bear family in order to survive. Nature, you have four seasons. When winter comes, nature sleeps. In the spring everything comes to life. In the summer, the fruit and vegetables ripen. Fall comes, that's when a lot of the people gather food for winter. And winter comes again. Nature sleeps. We have four colours: the sun is red; black is the sea; green is the mountain, the trees; blue is the sky, the rivers and the lakes. If you're an artist, you don't use many colours. You mostly use blue, black, red and yellow. We have four winds, four seasons. Everything is in four.

Since we formed the elders group ten years ago, we found drugs and alcohol was getting worse every year. Every conference we had we heard about it. We always say, "How are we going to tackle this? How are we going to get the justice or the police into our communities? Or are we going to go back to our old ways, where our people had control, the power in their own reserves?" They got hold of that person and made him do community work or something. He wasn't allowed to associate with the people for a while. In punishing him, he was put before the people and they decided his punishment. In some cases, the Longhouse Society "grabbed" these people. They still do that in some places. They go through a ceremony for three weeks. It is a very hard ceremony to go through to be an Indian dancer in the longhouse.

Some of those people who were grabbed don't go to the longhouse after the ceremony but many of them became workers to try to stop the use of drugs and alcohol. So it's working. It's getting better.

Us elders, we belong to many different religions. Some are Catholic, Anglican. So we say to ourselves, "Let's forget our religious differences. Let's go back to our old ways. Let's grab our children and start teaching them." We can go back to the sweat lodge like our people done before. I think this is what is really helping our young generation. Some are so bad that they have to put them in some rehab place to get them out of that habit. They have quite a few in British Columbia. Many of our grandchildren have been in there and come home after six weeks. It is very difficult when they come home because their families are drinking. It's the family in most cases that we need to get to sober up. Get them into the program. Otherwise, it's very hard for the young people who come back from treatment centres to stay off alcohol and drugs. We have to make this work. It is working. We have people working for the Alcohol Foundation but we have to get other people involved, the families, the community. I hear children in school just eleven or twelve years old are stoned. Where are they getting the drugs? That's the question us elders ask. We think our band councils should go ahead and make a bylaw to punish the suppliers, put them in jail.

I say, let's get serious. We have to give the police the authority to come on the reserve because they won't come if we don't do that.

A lot of our people are addicted to gambling. They run to bingo, Reno. Now they want to get a casino here. If they do that we'll have more people going to the band office saying they want welfare, I'm broke. They use the money up. Some win but most of them don't. Bingo is a good outing but sometimes you can overdo it.

I'm in the last cycle. People are coming to ask me, "What did you do in the past? What can we do in the future to teach our children?" We are faced with so many things, violence, drugs, alcohol. So we're going back to our culture, to the old ways;

taking our children back into the longhouse, taking them into the sweat lodge like they do in the prairies. It's coming back strong. The cycle of healing. We're healing a lot of people of the suffering when they went to school. Now they're that age, they're wondering what happened. Their cycle is coming back. They're giving themselves back to the Great Spirit. It is good to sit with an elder. It is good medicine for us. We like to talk. When the day is finished, I like to think I did something for today. Tomorrow is another day.

King of the Elders

I was King of the Elders. I was made the king, appointed up at the Nass River, Canyon City, in 1989. The following year we hosted the conference in North Vancouver on the Capilano Reserve. I told them in Canyon City that the hospitality of the Squamish Nation reached as high as Grouse Mountain. So from the time we left Canyon City we got together with the elders. We had meetings and we prepared. We really worked. We worked together what few elders we had that were able. I always tell them when we gather, sometimes twelve or fourteen, I look at them and say, "I'm going to give you a new name. Every time you get here I'm going to say I'm glad you're able to get here, so I'm going to call you Able." That's quite a thing with our elders. You know, a lot of them couldn't make it because they were sick, but I really was very impressed and I was proud of most of the elders who really got involved. This was to be the fourteenth gathering. I think the first one was held in Chilliwack. I've been to five. One in Terrace, one to Nass River, Musqueam, the one here and then in Alert Bay. The others I missed for some reason or another. I don't know why I missed them. I've always been invited. About nine years ago I went to the one in Terrace and the reception I got there was really something. I was the only one from the Coast Salish that went, but all the people from Ketchican and the Queen Charlotte Islands went as well. They had a good group. I was the grand marshall of the grand entry because I was the only one from the Coast Salish. That was quite a thrill for me, you know, to be part of that.

When we had the gathering here there was many things to do. You know, it takes a lot to involve an elder, but they heard and knew what we were trying to do, to invite all the elders from all over B.C. to participate, and so they got involved. I went ahead and had the education group do all the moccasin work. We had to arrange for billeting and everything else. The king and queen were automatically the chairman and chairlady. So that is how I was the chairman. Mabel Lewis was the Queen, and Pat Band, the co-ordinator of the Squamish elders, did a lot of work. May Harris co-ordinated a lot for the education group. She worked with the municipality so she knew where to approach people to get help and finances. That was a really important thing. We formed a group. We called ourselves the elders. We called it Síiyuxwa. That's the old elders. The old people. We call that our society. That's the name. We got ten thousand dollars from a special government program, and we had to use all that money from that day until a certain day, and when it was all spent we could reapply. But we did form our elders group and we continued on and have meetings to raise funds for ongoing events.

Something I believe in is the importance of the elders. People always keep saying, Why don't you go to the elders? Why don't you talk to the elders? Go and visit the elders and get them to tell you about some of the things of the past. They have been ignored so long that the elders just sit at home and nobody goes to them. Well, they are not going to talk if they feel that nobody's interested. So we formed our first elders group. I think that was the idea behind it — to get people talking. There are lots of good elders groups now. The Sto:lo Nation — they have a good group. Up the Nass River they have a good group. Also in the Interior. It was very difficult at first for us because we got about six reserves. We're all up in different areas so it's hard for the bunch to get together. We have to go and meet in Mission, Capilano and Squamish. We have these three places to go to get our group, and we had to keep them all interested.

At first the education group wanted to take control but we said no, and they said to us — well, you go ahead and we'll do what you want us to do for the conference. So we took control and that's the thing that I always remind them, that we, the elders, will decide what to do. We will decide whatever we want you to do, what we want the young people to do, and everybody's got to volunteer because we are raising the money ourselves and we're not getting anything out of it. We are just doing all this so that people will come here.

Many volunteered and we got committees together. All the women volunteered for the billeting of people in homes or hotels or whatever the case. They volunteered for the transportation. We had a lot of buses. They volunteered for the cooking. We had a lot of food and that was one of the main things. One girl volunteered to get all the youths who were going to do all the work serving. Then there was somebody else to look after the park and get what we needed, like tents and trailers and so on — whatever was necessary. It all worked out perfect because everybody had a job and the Squamish Indian Band Council had already put it on their record that they would pay for everything that we put in there, like the tents and so on. They were going to pay dollar for dollar for what we did so it just about worked out even. We raised twenty-six thousand dollars; the cost would be over fifty thousand dollars and the band paid the rest.

We had our program set so that the young people could take part. We followed our theme, "Elders Teach — Youth Reach." I told them, "We have gone too long in the wrong direction. We were a spiritual people. We paid great homage to our Creator and we must get back to that way of thinking. Spirituality, culture and language must be emphasized for our young people to know who they are. Education is the tool necessary for self-determination. We need lawyers, developers and managers, but it will take time. First of all, our young people need pride, and we hope this meeting will help them know who they are and where they come from."

So we had a lot of good elders who spoke and a lot of good young people who spoke. They talked about the life. They talked about drug and alcohol abuse. They talked about abuse and about elders' abuse and all this and you know, it really brought us together. A lot of us elders, we sit at home and nobody pays attention. We talked about this. We talked about how important it was to have someone to look after people who can't get around, like people on the wheelchair. There's a group of them that are on wheelchairs and have to have special care. That's the thing we want, some attention. Most of us now got nice homes. We built our homes. Now we're at the age when it's getting difficult. We need young people to come around and say, "Well, do you want your lawn cut?" and things like that. That's something I've been trying to tell the people ever since I was on council. I fought hard for the elders. That was before I got to be an elder. So now, you know, these meetings of the elders does create a lot of good feeling. It creates a lot of good friendship. It creates a lot of good things, not only for us here, but when the other elders go home they tell their people, "Well, we heard this and we'd like to carry on with it." You know, it's good when you go to these meetings. I've been to all these reserves and you'd be surprised how much the young people pay attention to the elders. They have their elders meeting and then the young do the lunch or dinner and take them out for a small trip. You know, it means a lot. Well, our meetings here went really good. We got the interest of the young people. We got the old people talking.

When they got here, well, my god, we got seven hundred elders that came here and we had to billet them and we had to feed them. It was good we had a lot of food. It took a lot to organize and control everything. The only problem we had was the first meal on the first day. We had a lot of young people but we needed to organize them and control things better. Everybody was walking around not sure what to do, so we gathered everyone together and said what had to be done, and if they didn't want to do it they had to get out. We divided them up and told them which tables to look after. We had to do that because we had between seven hundred and a thousand to serve. After that first meal everything went perfect. The boys would just go back and forth serving everyone at the table. They had three boys per table. They had it so well organized that one would serve the coffee, another the tea, another something else, and nobody complained.

I told them all when they first started, I said I don't want a lot of complaining. I'm going to do a lot of talking. Maybe I might get a little too bossy, but I said I know what I'm doing. I said I know because I've done this before. But I'm not going to force anybody. If anybody doesn't want to work with us, if anybody doesn't like to do the job with somebody telling you what to do, then I'm not going to force you. If you know the job well, that's good. If you can do it right I'll be happy. I'd let him do it, but if he makes one mistake and he doesn't listen, he's gonna get it. So that was how we keep them under control. That was the most important thing.

You always got to have one person that people can come to with their problems. You know, people say, "Si, what should we do? Or, are we doing okay? Are we doing the right thing?" In one case, two people were arguing and I got after the two of them and said, "You know what I am going to do with you two? I'm going to put you in the room and let you two argue it out, however you guys want to argue. If you want to fight it out, the one that comes out first, well, I'll know. But you want to forget any hard feelings." I don't want that. I don't want any hard feelings at all. We are all brothers and sisters and we're working in the longhouse and that's where our first elders worked together. There was a lot of harmony, everything, and everybody was happy, and that's what we are trying to teach our young people. There's not too many of us left that have gone through the old-time longhouse. I think there was only about four of us left out of the whole bunch.

We used to have a longhouse up Squamish. People had big times in the winter. Two of my grandmothers and some other people really knew how to gather people. They gave young people their names. There were marriages, death ceremonies, all of that. That's the thing we never forget, us elders. That's what I keep telling the young people. We got to remember our past. It's gonna be hard to revive it. It's gonna be the young ones coming up we want to teach our languages to. It's gonna be tough to teach. One or two really get it, but the rest, it's pretty hard. But at least we are teaching. Yeah, that's what we are getting all the money for. We are fighting for ways to do it in the proper way. A lot of young people don't believe in it. Well, they say everything's changing. That's why it's very difficult to revive the old tradition, the old customs. You can talk about it and you can tell the people and if they want to practise it, well, we'll let them go ahead, but they have got to do it in the proper way that was done in the old days. People from other reserves, their culture is different. Their customs, their songs and language are different. When they come to our longhouse they say, "Gee, this is something." The Coast Indians, most of them have longhouses pretty well, but you go up north and their longhouse is altogether different from ours. Their dances and everything is altogether different, but we recognize that's their way, that's their custom. That's the way they do their songs and dances. What's keeping a lot of harmony in all the reserves is that they are teaching their children the language and the dances. And it is wonderful to see them using all the beautiful clothing. When I went to Ottawa for the opening of that museum in Hull, I just couldn't believe it. The Nisga'as had over one hundred there. There were over eighty young boys and girls dancing in their beautiful clothes. This is what we all want to see, this kind of traditional clothing.

After our elders conference was all over the council came and told the committee they were going to give us a dinner to thank all the elders and I told that guy, I said, "I wish you would change that and invite all of us — give the workers the credit, because us elders, we were there just to be present, but the ones that should get the credit is all the committee and all the workers. They are the ones that should really be recognized." And the guy says, "That's good." That's what they want to hear, because they wanted us elders to decide what kind of meeting dinner they should put on. I said, "You councillors are giving it, so go ahead and do it, but please give the credit to all the workers, and we'll be there because we're the elders."

That elders gathering I believe has brought a lot of things to the elders. Before, they didn't seem to be as involved. They weren't so involved day to day. Now when they get up they say, "Oh yeah, we got a meeting coming next week. I'd better do something. I'd better make something." It's these little things that make a difference. Some of them like to make bread or something. When we said we wanted everybody to make something we could sell at a garage sale or a rummage sale, it was surprising what the elders, those that were able — remember that word "able" — made. So I feel the conference helped the whole community.

Any money we had left from the conference, we were going to give to the council, but they said they wanted us elders to keep whatever was left over for our trip to Alert Bay the following year. So that was good, because a lot wanted to get there. So then we started to raise money so that we could hire a big bus to go to Alert Bay. Once we got there everything was looked after, like our billeting and our food. The new king and queen were Agnes Cranmer and William Hunt. I don't know how old he is, but he must be in his eighties. Agnes was ninety-two, and I told her, I pray and hope that you'll be there next year when I come back.

All we had to pay was to get there and back. We continued to have meetings once a week. I am still chairman of the Squamish Elders, but I want someone else to take over. What I told them is now that I'm not a king any more, it is up to you guys to nominate a chairman. Whoever you want to.

I keep telling people now that when you get over eighty you can't say, "Well, I'm going to last another ten years." I'm just glad that I woke up this morning and saw the day because I don't know whether I'll see tomorrow. I just got to keep going day by day and keep my health and I'm trying to work hard and do everything.

I would really like to get a place where elders can get together. Not a museum but a cultural hall. That's what I would like to see, a place where all the Native elders can meet. We should have a cultural building with tapes and books written by the elders. Our future generations are going to go there and say, that was my grandfather and that was my great-grandfather.

The Role of the Elder: A Landmark Meeting

What to do next was the big question facing Indians of B.C. This was the question the Squamish people wanted addressed when we called the meeting of the elders in 1976. As this was a gathering to assist in solving a serious problem that had created disunity, disappointment, hardship and heartache among the Indians of British Columbia, the role of the elder kept coming up.

I think back on that landmark meeting with pride and some sorrow. I taped the proceedings and have presentations made by several speakers, so the record of the elders can be available to students, to the young people, so they will know what great leaders we have had.

I am sad that many of the elders who spoke at that meeting are gone and those who are alive are failing in health. I listen to the words of Guy Williams, Johnny Clifton, George Clutesi, Baptiste Richie and Clarence Joe. All were deeply concerned with the conditions of their people.

The meeting was held at what used to be the International Plaza Hotel, which is on Squamish land right near my house on the Capilano Reserve. The purpose of the meeting was to discuss an important issue. Many came without funding assistance from anywhere but their own pockets.

The Union of B.C. Indian Chiefs, the provincial organization representing the status Indians, had decided to reject all government funding. It was a brave move which at first had great support. However, before long the move resulted in hardship to many Indian people, particularly the unemployed, the disabled, the elderly and students. The well-meaning approach left the people bitter and uncertain.

It was an open meeting, and we encouraged everyone present to speak their minds, give their own views, express how they feel and say what they would like to see in the future. How do we wish to carry on?

Senator Guy Williams was the first to express his views. He made it clear at the outset that his remarks were as an Indian of B.C., not as a government representative or as a senator. Clarence Joe, the co-chairman of the meeting, introduced Guy Williams as a man who has been working for Indian people for many years, as president of the Native Brotherhood for fourteen years, previous to that as business agent for the Native Brotherhood, a man who has travelled across Canada, a pal and a colleague.

Guy referred to the meeting as a very symbolic one, one which was called by the Squamish people. He was proud to have worked under a Squamish leader in the past, namely the great Andy Paull. He said that no Indian in Canada could match Andy Paull's knowledge of government and Andy knew in his heart the needs of Indian people not only in B.C. but in Canada. "I was most fortunate to work for such a man," he remarked.

It was with pride that he referred to the development and leadership of the Native Brotherhood of B.C., an organization formed without government funds which demonstrated that Indians can manage their own affairs in today's society. This he related to what he perceived as the desire of Indian people, which was to be equal in this society.

He praised the efforts of the Nisga'a, as the first people to take up arms to protect their lands and to seek restitution through the courts in a settlement of land claims. He commented on the progress of the Federation of Saskatchewan Indians and the growing university enrollments.

Mainly, Guy spoke about the leadership of the organization known as the Union of B.C. Indian Chiefs, an organization that he helped to create. The UBCIC was criticized for being set on a political theme, following provincial election laws, forgetting the little people at home. Guy felt that the union had taken on a competitive value, which makes an individual out for himself rather than for the people.

The question he raised was, "Are we going to continue to hang our hats on a peg that has not worked? If not, what is the alternative for B.C.?" He called for deep co-operation of the people so that they might find a solution to their problem.

Johnny Clifton, the president of the Native Brotherhood at the time, stressed the need to respect elders, that no decisions should be made on behalf of Indians in B.C. without full consultation with the elders and individuals back home.

George Clutesi urged the group to deal with the problem without harsh words. He said, "We must ask ourselves how we can best get back together. What do we really think? What should we do? We the old-timers, old men and old women, are feeling bad because we seem to have been thrown aside because our usefulness has been considered to be at an end. Friends, in the old Indian tradition, in the old Indian philosophy, in the old Indian teachings, the older you get, the more you will be needed. The sooner the young people realize this, the sooner we can work together like one good family."

Charlie Peters of Cape Mudge said his pet program has always been education. He said, "Any person can go to school regardless of age. I thought my brain was a pound of cement, that I couldn't learn at my age. I found out differently. Education is how we prepare our people to deal with problems."

Following Charlie Peters's remarks, co-chairman Clarence Joe shared a little story about Charlie that had happened several years before at a Native Brotherhood conference. The delegates had been invited to some entertainment featuring actress Marie McDonald. They had presented her with a souvenir totem pole before her performance. At the end of her show, she came down the centre aisle looking for Guy Williams. He was president of the Native Brotherhood at the time. Anyway, Charlie Peters shouts out, "Right here." He's the one that got the kiss.

We were proud to be associated with the Native Brotherhood of B.C., which is still working for our people today.

Speaking at a Squamish powwow

With Ed Newman at the Quatell potlatch in Comox in 1989

With Emily at the time of our 50th wedding anniversary in 1984 (Steve Bosch/ *Vancouver Sun*)

On a friend's yacht in Indian Arm in 1992

Many of My Old Tillicums Are Gone

Many of my old tillicums are gone now. I used to get telephone calls from them, "How are you doing, Si? I'm doing fine." Now, they're not here today. I can't phone them. The funerals I attended were all important people. Some of them would have liked to have a funeral in the Indian way. I wondered what happened. They had that power. Yet, when they died, what did they do? They put him in a white man's cemetery. When one of my tillicums died on the Island, they didn't have any Indian ceremony of any kind, nothing. They put him in a white cemetery. His wife kept looking at me at the cemetery, expecting me to say a few words, but I couldn't. I felt it would have been out of place in a white man's cemetery. The same thing happened when another tillicum died. They wouldn't take him to his own reserve. He had to move out of the political and cultural movement of his reserve because the people went against him, so he moved to a nearby town. When he died, they wouldn't put him in the Indian cemetery at his reserve; instead, they put him in a white cemetery. He was the first person to be buried in that cemetery. That was quite a shock to me. It was fortunate that they had a gathering in a hall on his reserve with everybody there, all the pallbearers, and I was one of the forty honorary pallbearers. When they got in there, the first speaker they asked to speak was me. "Chief Simon Baker, we'd like you to come up." That's really something I treasure today because of the respect we held for one another. Once again I remember what my grandmother told me, "You're going to be a rich man, not in money, but in friends, a lot of good friends."

James Gosnell had the most beautiful Indian burial ceremony I've ever seen. It took a whole week. They have four tribes up there. Each tribe took part, all the clans. I enjoyed listening to those people talk. James Gosnell's dad, Eli Gosnell, and I were great friends from a way back even before I was married. I met him at the Skeena River at Claxton Factory. I believe James, his son, was just a young little boy then. It was unfortunate that I couldn't attend Eli's funeral because I had great respect for him.

I went to James Gosnell's funeral. My band paid my way, as an elder and a chief. So we took the trip to Terrace, stayed there overnight. We travelled to the Nisga'a Valley, through the historic lava fields. Several years before, Eli took me all over at a convention. He showed me where the lava stopped right at Canyon City. He said it was the year of the biggest run of humpbacks. He said that's the story that the humpback salmon stopped the lava. It's quite a canyon. You get to it by a swinging bridge. You just walk over. Nothing grows on the lava. One of the boys from my reserve was with us. He picked up a piece of the lava on our way by. He showed it to me the next day. I told him, "You better take that back, it's bad luck to take something away." The next day, he took it back right where he got it from, near a big plaque that tells how the mountain erupted and wiped out two Indian villages. I remembered the time my grandmother gave me hell when I took something from a historical place. Now I don't touch anything. I respect the culture, the history, I respect the Indian way, the tradition, the custom.

The next day, the funeral was in the church. They are Anglican and Salvation Army. So they had the families in the front. After the funeral, they carried the casket out through the village to the auditorium where his father, Eli, had carved a totem pole. They had a brass band there. They had a ceremony. Only the family clan members were allowed to talk. When they got through there, they packed him up a hillside road. They don't have a fenced-in cemetery. They bury their dead under a tree or anywhere on the side of the hill. Then they fence that grave in. It looks really nice. This is very, very interesting to me because their culture, their custom, are altogether different. They have four different clans, the eagle, the bear, the beaver, the wolf. If one family member dies of a different clan, they do the same thing. The next day, they collected money after they gave us a nice lunch of a bowl of soup and bread. When you feed eight to nine thousand people, that's a lot of work. The young girls that worked there, catered, came from the village. Everything was done so neatly, there was no problem. It was about six-thirty when they started collecting money. The first family came right up to the littlest grandchild, one hundred dollars, one thousand dollars, fifty dollars. Other families gave five dollars, ten dollars. It kept on and on. It was one or two o'clock before they got through collecting money.

6

THE FOUR CYCLES OF MY LIFE ARE ALMOST COMPLETE NOW

In My Heart I'm Proud and Happy

The four cycles of my life are almost complete now. From the day I was born, I did a lot of things as a family man, as a working man, as a Squamish man and as an elder. In my heart, I'm proud and happy about the things I have done.

I'm glad I listened and done things my grandmother taught me. I always retained the Indian way because of the early education with my grandmother. Today it is harder for young people to get that. Then there was a real role for the elder woman. Living with my grandmother, she taught me. She never had an education. She couldn't write her name yet she taught me how to survive. She taught me to listen. She taught me all the rules. She taught me how to respect my parents, neighbours, elders. After she died it all remained with me.

As I have mentioned many times, my grandmother was very dear to me. That's why I was very happy that a memorial pole was raised to honour her at the Capilano Suspension Bridge and Park, October 30, 1993.

Nancy Stibbard, who owns the Capilano Suspension Bridge and Park, asked two young men, James Lewis and Wayne Carlick, from the North Coast, to carve a totem pole to be placed by the new Story Centre that was just completed. When the young men saw the story of my grandmother, they asked me if they could dedicate the pole to my grandmother. It was wonderful to have Mary Capilano recognized this way. I told the boys, "Let's talk to Nancy about this." She liked the idea and together we planned the totem pole raising ceremony and potlatch.

Invitations were sent to many people to attend the ceremony. With the invitation, a short note on my grandmother was included. It said:

MARY CAPILANO

One of the most dearly loved local natives of this century, Mary Capilano was a remarkable woman of indefatigable spirit. She was well recognized on the North Shore, often seen picking berries on the banks of the Capilano River or digging for clams to sell to the Vancouver hoteliers at 5 cents a pound. She was born before native births were registered, probably around 1840. During her early years, her only contact with "the white man" was at the Hudson's Bay Company at Fort Langley. Mary witnessed the growth of Vancouver from a small settlement to a city of 300,000.

Mary fished for salmon in Burrard Inlet into her late eighties, refusing to stop until her concerned children confiscated her dugout canoe. Mary was the widow of Chief Joe Capilano, mother of Chief Mathias Joe Capilano and grandmother of Chief Simon Baker, who is conducting the blessing and raising ceremony today. Mary died in 1942, at the approximate age of 102. Her longevity was attributed to the herbal preparations of the medicine men and her steady pipe smoking!

At the ceremony, Nancy Stibbard spoke first. She welcomed everybody. Many people came. She said, "The story of the Capilano Suspension Bridge and Park includes the strong association formed with the Capilano Band. As you can see, Mary Capilano is represented here in a red cedar statue carved in 1930 by her son, Chief Mathias Joe; on her back is her papoose, the future chief. We are very pleased to raise a memorial pole to Mary Capilano today. Her presence has been with us not only with this statue but with the replica of her dugout canoe that she used daily to cross the inlet. As well, behind the pole is a beautiful photograph of Mary Capilano."

Nancy then turned the microphone over to me to bless the totem pole. She called me a long-time friend of the Capilano Suspension Bridge and Park.

When I was thinking of this special day, I thought of two things. One, it better not rain. I told the people, "This morning, I thanked the Great Spirit for the beautiful weather, this beautiful day. I listened to Norm Grohmann give the weather forecast last night, and if he said it was going to be bad, I had my bow and arrow ready to shoot him."

I was thinking also about Capilano. This park has our name. In Squamish it means "beautiful river." It is a river that fed our people for hundreds of years. They fished here for steelhead. This area is part of the traditional Squamish territory. I always remember August Jack telling me that he and his brother Willie helped put up the first suspension bridge in 1889. They used horses to drag the cables across the canyon, then they tied the cables to the trees and pulled them tight. The bridge was made from hemp rope and wood. They called it the laughing bridge because of the sound it made when the wind hit the hemp rope.

The bridge that's there now was built in 1956. It's the third wire bridge that was built so altogether they have built four suspension bridges since 1889. There is a book by Eleanore Dempster called *The Laughing Bridge*. It gives a good history of how our people from here were involved.

The Suspension Bridge has always been a great tourist attraction. The Squamish people got invited to celebrations. Dominic Charlie, August Jack and my uncle Mathias Joe always went there to perform. Now I'm alone, but they still ask me to go there. Rae Mitchell, Nancy's father, gave me a lifetime pass to get in there. I can also take my friends in free. One time, I took a whole busload. Another time, there were friends here visiting from New Zealand. Verna wanted to take them to the Suspension Bridge. I wasn't feeling well that day so I gave Verna my lifetime pass and wrote a note for her to show at the gate. I wrote, "Please let Verna Kirkness and her friends enter the park with my compliments as the holder of a lifetime membership." I signed it "Chief Simon Baker." I told Verna, "Let me know if they give you any trouble; I'll shut them down."

The owners of the Suspension Bridge and Park have always been reasonable to us Squamish people. I hope that after I'm gone one of my grandchildren will carry on, to come here to celebrate, to speak for our people. We are the Capilano family, the people of the river. We are part of that mountain.

With these thoughts, I began the blessing ceremony. I told the people, "We are known as the Capilano Creek family and I want to say that today, I am proud to be here with my family, my wife, my children, my grandchildren and great-grandchildren. Our youngest are the great, great-grandchildren of Mary Capilano. Mary Capilano raised me and this is where she brought me many times to pick berries."

I told my family to come and tap the pole before it was raised. I thanked the young men for carving the memorial pole. Then I sang the totem pole song.

I thanked everyone for coming to witness the raising of this totem pole dedicated to Mary Capilano, the most wonderful woman, called the Princess of Peace. "We say a prayer that your great, great, great-grandchildren can come and visit this area of our ancestors."

The carvers of the totem pole danced around the pole. They had their tools hanging on their outfits. They said, "This dance is a way of saying we're finished; we now make peace with the tree with this dance and spiritual song."

The celebration lasted a few hours. There was singing and dancing and a feast. The carvers gave away lovely prints commemorating the day and T-shirts.

In my heart I'm proud and happy that I could participate in this occasion, this special day when we all remembered my grandmother, Mary Capilano.

All my life, I didn't do anything to go against our people. I didn't do anything to go against white people. I tried to make it so people would enjoy themselves. I did things for my people. I wanted them to do things for themselves. I wanted others to do things for our people. Whenever I see them doing a good job, I compliment them. I congratulate them.

I hope that when the time comes for me to leave this good world of ours, I hope my mind will go saying, "I have no grudge, I did the things I wanted to do."

I'm glad to see people are getting more involved today. The powwow is starting to come back. Every powwow I go to I always get recognized as an elder. I have my outfit and I get up and dance. I get up and speak. That's one thing, I'm recognized wherever I go. I'm a good spokesman. People enjoy my talk. I tell a lot of things and I put a lot of humour in. That's what people enjoy, you know, the humour. I don't get too serious. I say, the day I get serious, well, something's going to happen to me, and I don't want that. I'm getting to the age now too when my body is not always ready to get up. But I don't like to turn anybody down when they ask me to do something. So when I have to go somewhere to do something, I get up and have a good bath and I get ready. When I get there I feel great. I always say that's a good medicine for me to go out and meet people, to get out and talk. I've met a lot of good people that I have enjoyed. So as long as I am able I will go on doing these things. Sometimes when I go out, I look at my lawn and gee, I say, I feel tired. But, my god, after a while I go out there and take my lawn mower and I do all my lawn and then I put on my hot tub and get in there, and after I relax I feel great. I feel that when I get something in my mind I deal with it. I don't sit and moan over everything. You know, that's the worst thing a person can do is feel sorry for himself, and that's the thing I always say. I'm still able. I still have my energy. Whatever little energy I have, I still have my mind, so I say to myself, "I better use it."

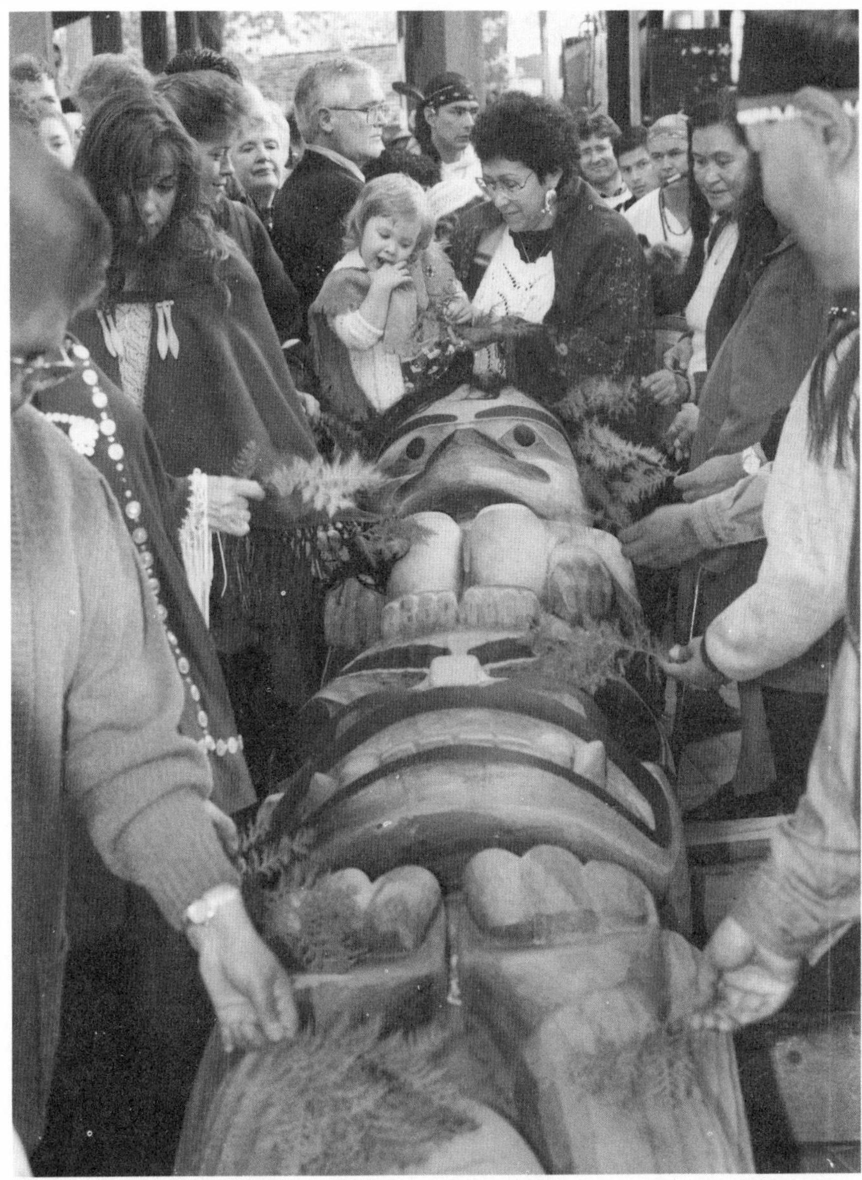

The totem pole carved by Wayne Carlick and James Lewis and dedicated to my grandmother, Mary Capilano, was raised at the Capilano Suspension Bridge in 1993. Here it is being blessed with cedar boughs by some of our children, grandchildren and great-grandchildren. (Denise Howard/*Vancouver Sun*)

With Emily at our 60th wedding anniversary in June 1994

Eight of our nine children were able to attend our 60th wedding anniversary celebration. *Left to right*: Peter, Charlie, Ken, Ron, Pauline, Barbara, Faye and Nancy. Priscilla was missing that evening.

As We Celebrate Our Diamond Wedding Anniversary

On June 7, 1994, it was sixty years ago that Emily and I got married. I am now eighty-three years old and Emily is seventy-nine. As we sit comfortably in our home, we are happy. We now have four generations in our immediate family. As Emily said, the sixty years went by so fast.

I thank Emily for living with me for sixty years; for our nine children, thirty-four grandchildren and twenty-four great-grandchildren. The good times were the many birthday parties, the Christmas celebrations, having plenty of food, having a comfortable home and enjoying ourselves as a family. I wish all our married life could have been for "better" and not for "worse."

I remember the day Emily and I got married. She had to buy the wedding ring, and we had to spend our first night as husband and wife in Gertie's bedroom that she gave up for us. Times were tough; I had no money to speak of. So the vow "for better or for worse" really meant something for us right from the start.

I am sorry that Emily had to live with me through some tough times, "for worse." Times when I spent more time on sports, organizing powwows, and travelling. All the things I did, I didn't realize at the time how much hardship I had put on her. She was the one that made things livable, made things for our children and for the home. Even when I was sick, she was able to carry on. When I was away many times, she was able to carry on. There are so many things I would like to make up to her.

We've had our hard times; we've had our good times. I know that there were times she felt like leaving me, but the children kept us together. For me, there was never a moment, there was never a time that I ever thought of leaving her. She never gave me a reason to except for bawling me out once in a while, but I had it coming.

They say a woman can make or break a man. Well, Emily made me. With that, I say to her, "I thank you, Emily, thank you for all you have done, thank you for your love and friendship, for better or for worse."

I was very, very proud that I was able to sit with my wife to celebrate sixty years of marriage. The Squamish people, our people, put on a great celebration for us at our recreation centre. When they escorted us in, I couldn't believe that all these people had come to honour us.

All our family was there, the Bakers' side and the Rivers, Emily's family, our children, grandchildren and great-grandchildren, and friends, both Natives and non-Natives. I knew we were in for a wonderful evening.

Emily and I received the highest honour that can be given in our society. It was the Swai-swai, a ceremonial mask dance. I was very proud and very emotional during the dance. What came to my mind was what I had seen years ago when I went around here and there with my uncle Mathias Joe, August Jack and Dominic Charlie. I saw the Swai-swai done quite a few times in them days.

Now, our people are working on getting it back. Barbara Charlie was the one who organized the ceremonial mask dance. I said, "Thank you, Barbara." She said, "Don't thank me, I want to thank you for teaching me, for keeping the song that belonged to my dad." Her dad was Dominic Charlie. I was glad to help her along over the years, to encourage her to learn the ways of her father. Then she taught her children and they were initiated into the Swai-swai. It was good to have our children and grandchildren take part, be there to witness this sacred ceremony. It was an experience I don't think they will ever forget.

The speeches that evening were really something. When my nephew Chief Joe Mathias spoke, I felt very emotional, because I know what he has had to go through. He started working for his people at a young age. I'm proud of him; he's a strong leader.

Everything went so nicely that evening. I know everybody who came enjoyed the ceremony and the delicious meal.

When you've been married and had a family for sixty years, you think a lot about your children, their children and all your friends. Many thoughts have been going through my mind lately. I would like to tell the grandchildren, all young people, "Get your education and keep away from alcohol and drugs. Visit your grandparents, offer to help them, mow their lawns or something."

To our many friends, our tillicums, I want to say that some of the greatest moments in my life are at gatherings when I am with all my friends that I have associated with politically and culturally. Our anniversary night was one of those times. I thank them for coming. Their presence there, at our sixtieth wedding anniversary, was important to Emily and me. We have always tried to work with and be friends with all people, Native or non-Native, from our village or anywhere in the world.

Some of them, I worked with them or their fathers and grandfathers to challenge education, to challenge land claims, to keep our culture strong. For me this has been my life for over fifty years. We worked to get our foot in the door and to keep it open for the young generation. Now it has come. I hope our young people will do the right thing so that we can live as good self-governing communities. I'm proud that I stood with my colleagues when we challenged Ottawa.

My advice to everyone is, through the good years and the bad, never give up. I never said I wanted to give up, to throw everything away, even when things seem to be going wrong. I always believed we could do things. Many years ago, I dreamed we'd have a great big building for sports. Well, it's there now.

We have it. It's been my way to think, "Go and show them; show them you can do it. Even if you don't win, do your best. Never hesitate, you can do it."

I believe we should share, get up and speak, do the moccasin work, talk to the people — communicate. Our culture is something I have always respected. As the elders before me, I loved to demonstrate what our songs and dances mean. We have to keep doing this, to be proud of who we are, to show our different Nations with our regalia. We have button blankets, cedar bark clothes, buckskins. We have all these things. We have to teach our children that we are the salmon people, the canoe people; that we must respect the animals because of all the important things we get from the animals, all the different feathers we get from the birds, all the things that grow on the mountain, how we use the bark. It's there. We have to go out and get our children to understand so they will use it, not destroy it.

There is so much good we can do. I always say, "Never criticize your neighbour until you have walked a full day in his moccasins." That's what I believe. Don't say anything if you're not going to say anything good. It's better to keep it in silence. That's the way I was taught. Always help your neighbour. I think that's what has worked for me all my life.

I thank the Great Spirit for my friends. I thank the Great Spirit for our children, grandchildren and great-grandchildren.

Men huyḵw na wa en sníchim, síy̓am̓, síiyay̓, en s7eḵwlí7tel.

(This is all I have to say, chiefs, friends, my family.)